Soviet-Era A

The Final Three Decades

CHRISTOPHER BUCKLEY

HISTORIC COMMERCIAL AIRCRAFT SERIES, VOLUME 1

Back cover image: We can hopefully rely on the military and diverse government agencies to keep various old Soviet transports in service for a while yet. Operated by the Russian Air Force, well-travelled An-30 '01' is at Zhukovsky in July 2017, taking a break from its usual 'Open Skies' spying missions across Europe. It was then approaching its 40th birthday.

Title page image: Not renowned for its great beauty, the rugged An-12 nevertheless wins top marks for longevity. In early 2021, after resolving a few regulatory issues, Ukrainian operators were back flying 50-year-old An-12s again on worldwide cargo charters. Bulgaria was also a haven for An-12s for decades. Two Balkan Bulgarian aircraft are awaiting their next assignment in Sofia in April 1994.

Contents page image: Glass noses were a feature of many Soviet airliner designs. It must have been great to be a navigator up in the nose of a Tu-134, the Siberian steppes unfolding beneath your feet. Tu-134A-3 RA-65783, recently retired by Aeroflot, heads a glass-nosed line-up of three other Tu-134s, an Il-76 and an An-12 at Moscow's Zhukovsky airfield in August 2009.

Dedication

This book is dedicated to the memory of Brian Dunn: historian, enthusiast, a great friend and a wonderful man. A long-time manager with Air Canada in Toronto, Brian was always happy to be around Soviet airliners – as long as he stayed firmly on the ground at YYZ.

Published by Key Books
An imprint of Key Publishing Ltd
PO Box 100
Stamford
Lincs PE19 1XQ

www.keypublishing.com

Acknowledgements

My very grateful thanks go to Yefim Gordon, Dmitry Komissarov and Sergey Komissarov, for their incredible series of detailed books on Soviet aircraft. If you didn't know that U-30MES-10 and UT-32 compounds are used to seal the joints of the Tu-134's six integral fuel tanks in the wing torsion box, then Dmitry's book on the Tu-134 is just for you. I am also very grateful to Peter Hillman, Stuart Jessup, Adrian Morgan, Tony Morris, Guus Ottenhof and Michael Roch, and their outstanding 'Soviet Transports' reference books, which are an amazing feat of research. Thanks also to Tony Merton Jones and *Propliner* magazine, *Irish Air Letter*, *Aviation Letter*, *Russian Aviation Insider*, Vladislay Filev, Roman Pakhomov, Tom Singfield, Max Kingsley-Jones, Benoit Machefert, Julien Franiatte, Maria Shlyakhtova, Quentin Hebrard, Dave Bougourd, Andrey Martirosov, Andrew Harvey, Jon Jackson, Anita Baker and Jessica Brown.

Typeset by SJmagic DESIGN SERVICES, India.

Contents

Like so many Soviet airliners, the Tu-154 was not short on charisma. Tu-154A LZ-BTE was an early aircraft delivered to Balkan Bulgarian in the summer of 1974, and later converted to a Tu-154B. It is sharing the ramp in Sofia with Tu-134A-3 LZ-TUZ in September 1994.

The indomitable Tupolev trijet enjoyed a long production run. Tu-154M RA-85833, the last Tu-154 ever built, was delivered new to Ural Airlines no less than 28 years after Balkan proudly received -BTE. It is seen here powering away from Moscow's Domodedovo Airport in August 2009.

Introduction

Many years ago, the author was sitting patiently in the sweltering cabin of a Tupolev Tu-154B-2 belonging to Tarom, the Romanian airline. We had been on the ground in Cairo for well over an hour. There had been no announcement to explain why our departure to Bucharest was delayed. The Tupolev's air conditioning was struggling to keep up with the Egyptian heat in high summer, and the unique odours in a Soviet-era airliner – a heady mix of nuclear-grade industrial disinfectant, oil, well-used cabin furnishings, long-forgotten galley spillages and other smells of dubious origin – seemed even more pronounced than usual.

Over and above the noise from the APU and labouring air-conditioning system, every few minutes there would be a series of loud clangs under the right wing. Somebody was clearly at work with a large hammer. It sounded as if a blacksmith was under the wing, hammering something into shape on a giant anvil. Maybe he was making a new strut, right there on site, for the Tupolev's impressive six-wheel undercarriage assembly.

Another hour passed, with more intermittent clanging. From the vantage point of a window seat, our captain could be seen down on the ramp, heading for the wing. The flight engineer and two EgyptAir mechanics emerged from under the leading edge, looking extremely hot and bothered. The body language out in the heat did not look encouraging. There was much gesticulating and wringing of hands. The captain could be seen shaking his head. He stared at the ground for a long few seconds. Then, clearly to the surprise of his audience, he pointed back to the cockpit and issued a command.

Whatever was wrong with the Tupolev, flight RO242 was going to depart anyway. Fifteen minutes later, we were treated – three times – to the distinctive, mournful howl of the air starter as each Kuznetsov NK-8-2U turbofan spooled up. No other engine, anywhere, makes that noise. With a burst of power the Tu-154, very much alive, headed for the runway.

Maybe it is not everyone's cup of tea, but for some of us (well, perhaps very few of us) there was an incomparable mystique and magic about flying in Soviet-era aircraft with operators of the day. The noises and entire in-flight experience could not be replicated anywhere else.

The first of 12 Tu-154Bs was delivered to Tarom in 1976. They had all been retired by 1997. Tu-154B-1 YR-TPB, in the latest colours, is seen taxiing past a company BAC One-Eleven in Brussels in August 1995.

There was always that nagging feeling that something might go very wrong. Over the winter of 1973–74, EgyptAir itself had taken delivery of eight early-production Tu-154s. The fleet lasted a matter of months before being withdrawn from passenger service, pending resolution of alleged safety issues with the electric, fuel and fire suppression systems. One of the aircraft then crashed on a training flight near Cairo, and the Tu-154's career in Egypt was abruptly over. The passengers on flight RO242 today were certainly oblivious to the big Tupolev's unfortunate association with Cairo Airport.

Although some kind of serviceability issue had clearly not been fixed, as we taxied out there was the reassuring sight of two Tarom flight attendants already lying down for a sleep across two rows of seats in the passenger cabin. They were clearly at ease with the captain's unexpected decision to depart. Our Tu-154 roared skywards over the desert, with a few unexpected turns and power changes for good measure during the climb.

The possibility of such adventures has now, sadly, almost come to an end. The once-great fleet of Tupolevs, Ilyushins, Yaks and Antonovs from Soviet times will soon be just a distant memory. The majestic four-engined Ilyushin 62 has seen very limited commercial passenger service since 2011. The last revenue flight of the mighty 350-seat Ilyushin 86 took place in the same year. The Russian airline Alrosa had the honour of flying the last passenger flights (in Russia at least) of both the hugely successful Tu-134, in May 2019, and the Tu-154, in October 2020. The combination of high operating costs, new noise and emission standards, spare parts availability and old age has not helped these noisy, smoky veterans of another era.

All of these enigmatic types are still in limited military use, so have not vanished quite yet. In recent years, North Korea's Air Koryo has been enterprising enough to arrange special flights for aircraft enthusiast groups in its few airworthy Ilyushins and Tupolevs, but it is unsure whether it will ever happen again.

A routine summer afternoon at Prague's Ruznye Airport back in July 1992, when western aircraft were in the minority and CSA's impressive fleet still included 32 Soviet-built jetliners. Tu-134A OK-EFK is on the move behind Il-62M OK-KBK.

Despite their great age, fortunately many more of the Antonov turboprops are still flying. The diminutive Yak-40 trijet is also still around, along with a few last examples of the much bigger Yak-42, an aircraft with a troubled past that has haunted its career in Russia.

The subject of Soviet aviation, the airlines that have operated Soviet-built aircraft and the history of the aircraft themselves is truly vast. It is far beyond the scope of this modest book – there were around 400 new airlines in Russia alone during the 1990s. There is enough history with Soviet airliners in Sharjah, Iran and China – and even Latin America – to merit four completely separate books.

The intention in the next few pages is to celebrate the final three decades of the great Soviet airliner and the airlines themselves, using images to provoke a few anecdotes, facts and figures. Of course, we have to include a few famous freighters, such as the An-12 and Il-76.

Why three decades? Because the fall of the Soviet Union, in December 1991, seems a logical place to start. The timeframe allows us a look at the surprisingly few airlines that were actually flying Soviet-built airliners at the time. One major operator, Interflug, had already disappeared the year before after the unification of Germany. We can then move right into the incredible years that followed, when Antonovs, Ilyushins, Tupolevs and Yaks were unleashed everywhere imaginable, with new airlines coming and going within a few weeks. Everything started to calm down at the turn of the millennium, and much more so from 2010 to 2020.

For over 60 years, An-12s have never been shy about making their presence felt on take-off. Its four smoking Ivchenko AI-20M turboprops at full bore, Atran's RA-93913 departs from Moscow's Domodedovo Airport in August 2009.

Soviet ambassadors around the world, Aeroflot's flagship long-haul Il-62s ventured far and wide for three decades. Il-62M CCCP-86517 is arriving in Havana early one morning in September 1991, just as two Cubana An-24s are being prepared for their first flights of the day.

Sister ship CCCP-86523 was seen in Toronto in June 1989, again sharing space with Cubana as Tu-154M CU-T1265 taxies to its stand.

Chapter 1

The Wild Nineties

At the beginning of the 1990s, few airlines apart from Aeroflot operated sizeable fleets of Soviet-built aircraft on international passenger schedules. Usually for political reasons, they had all long been captive customers for the Soviet airliner industry. Depending on their requirements, the airlines would have been assigned long-range Ilyushin Il-62s, typically with about 150 seats; medium-haul, 150-seat Tupolev Tu-154s; shorter-haul 76-seat Tu-134s; and then An-24s or Yak-40s for local routes. The 'customers' were Aeroflot, LOT, Malev, Balkan Bulgarian, CSA, Tarom, Vietnam Airlines, Mongolian Airlines, Cubana, the new Chinese airlines that were emerging from CAAC and a few smaller entities.

All these airlines, Aeroflot included, had already launched, or were about to launch, their first forays into Western-built equipment. This would mean either direct orders from Airbus or Boeing, contracts with leasing companies, or (in the case of Cubana) wet leases from other airlines.

When the Soviet Union fell in December 1991, the fleet of Soviet-built aircraft worldwide was the largest it had ever been. From the 32-seat Yak-40 to the heavyweight Il-86 widebody, in 1991 there were around 3,500 Soviet airliners that could be deemed operational. 3,000 of these were with the 35 directorates of Aeroflot alone, scattered across the 22 million square kilometres of the Soviet Union.

There were still more to come. Twenty-seven years after its first flight, the long-serving Ilyushin Il-62 remained in limited production in Kazan. Il-86s were still being built in Voronezh, and the first Il-96 had only flown two years earlier. Tu-154s continued to roll slowly off the line in Samara, as did Yak-42s in Saratov.

Initially, the outlook seemed bleak. Many operators were developing a taste for fuel-efficient Western aircraft, and engines that would stay on the wing for years rather than a few months. Aeroflot's future was uncertain, and the once-monolithic airline was fragmenting into many parts.

It was unclear how all these aircraft would be supported, and there were doubts about spares availability and overhauls in the future. In Soviet times, for example, many Tu-134s would usually fly to one of two designated Tu-134 'centres of excellence' for major overhauls and rework: Minsk or

There were close to 90 Soviet-built airliners in Bulgaria alone in 1992. Long line-ups of under-utilised aircraft were always a feature at airports in the Soviet bloc. Here in Sofia in April 1994, a visiting Aeroflot Tu-154M has parked in front of four idle Balkan Tu-154s. LZ-BTU, with the red tail, had been on lease to Palair Macedonian following the break-up of Yugoslavia.

Rostov-on-Don. However, Minsk was now in newly independent Belarus. Would the Belarussians continue this tradition? Who would take over the Rostov plant? Was there even a viable business case for Tu-134 maintenance far into the future?

Fortunately, a good dose of newly found entrepreneurship, very cheap aircraft and a huge pool of trained pilots and engineers combined to confound the sceptics. It was estimated that Aeroflot had 600,000 employees in 1991. The vast majority of them had only ever known how to work in, or around, aircraft and engines that had been built in their homeland.

The limited operator base in 1990 expanded beyond anyone's wildest dreams. The speed with which some of Aeroflot's regional directorates and their fleets ended up in the hands of new owners was remarkable. Some aircraft were just seized or 'appropriated' where they stood, or picked up for next to nothing at privatisation auctions. There were certainly some wild stories to be told, with a new breed of airline managers that came out of nowhere.

Aeroflot's remarkable organisational structure in Soviet times undoubtedly helped the reassignment of aircraft and technical facilities once the USSR was no more. In 1991, Aeroflot was made up of 21 autonomous Civil Aviation Directorates (CADs) across Russia (including three separate operations at Moscow's Sheremetyevo, Domodedovo and Vnukovo airports), another 11 CADs in the republics that were to become the Commonwealth of Independent States and another three in Estonia, Latvia and Lithuania.

Each CAD might have had several United Air Detachments (UADs) at different bases within the directorate. In turn, each UAD might have more than one 'Flight', depending on how many aircraft types were assigned to this outlying base. Some flights might then comprise two or more squadrons. So, If you were running your squadron of An-24s somewhere in Siberia, you would be far down the hierarchy (and very far away) from the big bosses in Moscow.

Looking just like any other Aeroflot Tu-134, Tu-134A-3 CCCP-65074 was assigned to the North Caucasian CAD when it was delivered in late 1977. It spent all its life based in Mineralnye Vody. Now RA-65074, it is seen heading home from Athens in May 1995, not yet repainted in KMV colours (see page 83).

As far away from Moscow as you could possibly go in the Soviet Union (or today in Russia), the story of one old Antonov would be similar to that of many more.

An-24RV CCCP-46616 emerged from the Svyatoshino factory in Kiev in 1973, fitted out with 48 seats and ready for action. Aeroflot's chief aircraft allocator (if that is the right term) in Moscow promptly sent the little Antonov off on a long ferry flight to its new home with the Magadan CAD, eight time zones and 6,000km away from Moscow in the far eastern corner of Siberia.

The local directors in Magadan then sent 46616 another 1,500km (and another time zone) to the northeast, to the Anadyr United Air Detachment on the remote Chukotka peninsula. The An-24, resplendent in its special high-visibility red 'polar' colours, was now under the responsibility of Aeroflot's 150th Flight, 2nd Squadron in Anadyr. It would spend the rest of its Aeroflot career in this remote, inhospitable part of the world.

As an aside, on rare occasions, 46616 would be privileged to visit the United States. Not many An-24s have ever done that. It would take trade and friendship delegations over the forbidding Bering Sea (and International Date Line) to Alaska. Anchorage is just slightly further away from Anadyr than Magadan. The Antonov is seen on a murky winter day in Anchorage in March 1990, adorned with the US flag for the special trip. It is not known if Aeroflot's top management in Moscow was ever aware that one of its aircraft was flying around emblazoned with the Stars and Stripes.

So, what happened to this An-24 after the fall of the Soviet Union? Well, like so many local and regional assets in Aeroflot's massive structure, it stayed exactly where it was. The 'CCCP-' in the Antonov's registration was changed to 'RA-', for Russia. The Anadyr UAD gradually evolved into a new airline, Chukotavia. In 2020, RA-46616 was still flying stolidly around the wilderness of northeast Siberia, just as it had always done for an amazing 47 years.

In 1992, there were other similar stories across Russia. In the new Commonwealth of Independent States – Armenia, Azerbaijan, Georgia, Kazakhstan, Kyrgystan, Moldova, Tajikistan, Ukraine and Uzbekistan – the local Aeroflot assets were taken over exactly where they stood. New airlines like Air Moldova started up, almost overnight, with whatever aircraft had been flying from Aeroflot's bases in their newly independent countries. For Air Moldova this meant inheriting Tu-134s and Tu-154s from Aeroflot's 269th Flight in Kishniev (Chisinau), along with An-24s and An-26s from the 407th Flight.

Across Russia and the Commonwealth of Independent States (CIS), there was little time to be wasted with the niceties of repainting aircraft or making changes to the Aeroflot cabin layouts. In any case, the infrastructure was simply not available to repaint hundreds of aircraft all at once. For several years there were countless aircraft flying around with the basic Aeroflot cheatline, with new airline names and logos hastily applied over the large Aeroflot titles and Soviet flag. Some airlines, like Dalavia in distant Khabarovsk, never managed (or maybe never wanted) to move away from the basic Aeroflot colours.

Nevertheless, there was immediately lots of painting and refurbishing business out there. Tu-134B-3 CCCP-65146 has been stripped down before ferrying from Russia to Shannon, Ireland, to be painted for Latvia's newly formed Latavio in July 1992.

Ilyushin 86 CCCP-86104, seen visiting Toulouse in December 1992, symbolises the rapid evolution in the first year of the non-Soviet world. This aircraft had been delivered in the summer of 1989 from the factory in Voronezh to Aeroflot's 65th Flight at Moscow's Vnukovo Airport, part of the Vnukovo Civil Aviation Production Association.

Proudly accepting another gleaming 350-seat Il-86 into its fleet, the Aeroflot team in Vnukovo would not have begun to imagine that its big Ilyushin would wear the names of three different airlines just three years later, let alone have the name 'Ramsi' casually painted on the nose. It would have been even more surprised that the Il-86 would fly for Transaero, the first of Russia's new private airlines (and a future competitor for Aeroflot) and in turn for Greenair, a Turkish charter airline.

When the Soviet Union fell in December 1991, Aeroflot was operating close to 95% of all the Soviet airliners in commercial service. Airlines within the Soviet Union's sphere of influence were operating almost all the rest. There were also many more aircraft in Aeroflot colours that served with the military. The Tupolev Tu-134, which first flew in July 1963, was a core part of the Aeroflot fleet from 1967 to 2007. Of the 852 Tu-134s built, 600 flew for Aeroflot. Usually configured with between 68 and 76 seats, it was rugged and reliable. Despite the harsh operating conditions and primitive airfields in remote parts of the Soviet Union, the safety record of the -134 was relatively good.

You would always know when a Tu-134 was on the move. The distinctive, urgent whistle of the Tu-134's Soloviev D-30 engines when it was taxiing set it apart from any other jetliner. The fighter-like roar on take-off was spectacular. Unfortunately, the roar ended up playing a big part in the Tupolev's downfall, as the Tu-134 failed to meet (by a big margin) all the new ICAO noise and emissions limits that came into force in 2002. Tu-134A-3 CCCP-65783, which we saw earlier in retirement (Page 3), is whistling its way onto stand in Prague in July 1992.

The imposing Tu-154 trijet had around twice the capacity of the Tu-134. First flown in October 1968, no fewer than 1,026 were built, and 627 flew with Aeroflot between 1972 and 2009.

For most of 1992, much of the Aeroflot fleet still carried a 'CCCP-' (SSSR) registration and wore the Soviet flag. It would take time to repaint the Russian flag on such a huge fleet. Tu-154M CCCP-85648 is arriving in Nairobi in June 1992, and is still looking very Soviet.

The elegant Ilyushin 62 had been the backbone of Aeroflot's long-haul fleet since the late 1960s, when it displaced the awesome Tupolev 114 turboprop as the airline's new flagship. Aeroflot might have been proud to introduce a new long-haul jet, but the original Il-62 could not begin to rival the Tu-114 when it came to range capability. First flown in January 1963, the original Il-62 with Kuznetsov NK-8-4 engines entered service with Aeroflot on the important domestic route from Moscow to Alma Ata (now Almaty) in September 1967. Depending on the cabin arrangement, a three-class Aeroflot Il-62 might have as few as 132 seats. High-density layouts could accommodate up to 180 passengers. An estimated 295 Il-62s were built in total, of which 213 flew with Aeroflot.

In 1992, the much-upgraded Soloviev-powered Il-62M was still flying most of Aeroflot's long-haul schedules. CCCP-86553 is landing in Shannon for a fuel stop in October 1992. It is still in its Soviet marks. Shannon was an Aeroflot stronghold for many years, with most transatlantic services stopping there (as we will see later).

The beefy Ilyushin 86 looked impressive, made a lot of noise and was popular with passengers. Designed in the 1970s to demonstrate that the Soviets could also build a prestigious widebody airliner, it first flew in 1976 and entered service in 1980. The Il-86 won acclaim as a great airframe, but was let down by its engines. With no better technology available that offered enough power, its Kuznetsov NK-86s were just scaled-up versions of the NK-8s on early Il-62s and Tu-154s. Fuel consumption was high (ten tonnes an hour), climb performance was modest, and range very limited. A total of 106 were produced, a small production run by Soviet standards. CCCP-86066 is heaving its way skywards from Shannon in July 1992.

Moving on to the other established players in the Soviet airliner world, we will start with Malev in Hungary – and the diminutive Yak-40.

In Soviet times, Aviaexport, the marketing arm for the nation's aircraft industry, tried hard to find buyers in the West for its large and diverse portfolio of aircraft. The Aviaexport teams were not very successful, but they made an extra effort with the 27-32 seat Yakovlev 40. There was no equivalent to this robust, go-anywhere trijet in the West. First flown in October 1966, five years later the Yak was visiting unlikely places such as the grass runway at Portsmouth Airport, England, in the hope of export sales success with modest carriers like JF Airlines. No fewer than 1,011 Yak-40s were built in Saratov (in Ukraine) before the last one was delivered in 1980.

In 1992, Malev, the Hungarian national airline, had already introduced 737s and 767s, but still operated two Yak-40s, six Tu-134As and 12 Tu-154B-2s. The Yaks were comparatively short-lived in the fleet, and leased from Aeroflot from 1991 to 1993. Here HA-LJA is seen arriving in Vienna from Budapest in June 1992. Not noted for its speed or climb performance, the Yak-40 was ideal for this kind of short sector, just over 200km.

The Tu-134 served Malev in various guises for a remarkable 30 years, and the Tu-154 28 years. Malev stayed resolutely with the Kuznetsov-powered Tu-154B-2, and – unlike its neighbours CSA and LOT – never operated the more capable and updated Tu-154M, powered by Soloviev D-30KU turbofans. HA-LCU, seen here at Heathrow in July 1994, proudly carried 'Alitalia Partner' titles. It seemed a strange alliance at the time. Malev flew its last Tu-154 service, from Prague to Budapest, in March 2001. The airline stopped flying altogether in early 2012.

Up the road in Poland, LOT was a latecomer to the Tu-154. The first of 14 150-seat Tu-154Ms was delivered in 1986, but just eight years later the fleet had been ousted by new Boeings. This short service life contrasted with LOT's long 30-year experience with the faithful Il-18 turboprop, which the -154s were to replace. SP-LCI, here on a charter to Toulouse in April 1992, only flew with LOT for five years. Like its sister ships, low-time-LCI (which went on to Samara Airlines) was eagerly snapped up by new Tupolev-hungry airlines in Russia and the CIS.

Almost all LOT's sizeable Soviet-built fleet was retired rapidly in the early 1990s. This included the seven remaining Il-62Ms, which in turn had replaced early-build Il-62s that dated back to 1972. LOT lost its very first Il-62 in a fatal accident near Warsaw in 1980, and – in Poland's worst-ever air disaster – an Il-62M seven years later, also outside Warsaw. The accidents had an eerie similarity. They both involved loss of control after fire in the rear of the aircraft destroyed the cables to the tail and horizontal stabiliser. Interflug had lost its first Il-62 in similar circumstances in 1972. Despite the aircraft's patchy reputation in Poland, Air Ukraine was a willing buyer for the Il-62Ms in early 1992. SP-LBC is landing in Toronto in February 1990.

Like LOT, CSA in Czechoslovakia (as it was then) came into the 1990s with Il-62Ms, Tu-154Ms and Tu-134As anchoring the fleet. Unlike LOT, and even if two Airbus A310s had arrived and 737s were on the way, CSA was content to keep its Soviet aircraft a while longer. CSA had been an early customer for the 'A' variant of the Tu-134, which was 2.1 metres longer than the original Tu-134. It offered higher operating weights and an extra row of seats, for a total of up to 76 passengers.

Back in 1971, Tupolev had proposed an export version of the Tu-134A with weather radar in the nose, and CSA's 14 aircraft all had the new, modern 'radar nose'. OK-EFK is resplendent at Prague in July 1992, with a Tu-154M in the older red colours in the background. CSA was also late to the Tu-154 party, with seven Tu-154Ms joining the fleet from 1988. The first three were sold off in 1992, but the last four stayed on until the end of the decade.

Not all the Tu-134s were quite so resplendent on this warm summer day. Hidden away behind CSA's maintenance base on the far side of the airfield, it was close to the end for OK-CFC. Only three of CSA's 14 Tu-134As went on to other customers (in Bulgaria and Georgia). After 26 years of accident-free service and almost 15 million happy passengers, the rest of the aircraft were simply out of hours, and gracefully retired from service. After its retirement in November 1988, CSA's first Tu-134, OK-AFA, had been ferried to the Soviet Union for close examination and testing to destruction. It had flown almost 20,000 cycles, and no Aeroflot aircraft had come close to such a figure. The last CSA Tu-134A service was flown in December 1992.

CSA had been the first export customer for the Il-62 back in 1969, but had leased aircraft the previous year from Aeroflot to gain experience on the type. Nine of the early Il-62s were followed by six Il-62Ms, which flew on until October 1994. OK-JBJ, seen in July 1992, had been repainted in yet another new variation of the CSA colours following a short lease to Malev the previous year.

The Il-62 was certainly more popular in the Czech Republic than in Poland. There seemed to be a frenzy of local buyers waiting to take over CSA's Ilyushin flagships. New operators like Bemoair, Georgia Air Prague and Ensor Air were soon flying surprised Czech holidaymakers around the Mediterranean. However, none of them lasted very long. The infrastructure and costs involved in flying small one- and two-aircraft fleets of ageing Soviet aircraft were prohibitive to say the least. By the middle of 1998, the Czech Republic had finished its long association with the Il-62 – almost 30 years.

At the other end of the scale, CSA's Yak-40s were on their way to retirement after some 15 years of service. CSA started operating ATR-72s in 1992. The ATR might have been a turboprop, but it had more than twice the number of seats, was slightly faster, boasted a quieter cabin and burned just 60% of the fuel of the little jet it would replace. And unlike the Yak, the ATR did not leave a long trail of black smoke on take-off. In July 1992, OK-HEP had recently been retired in Prague.

The iconic Ilyushin 18 turboprop was still going strong in the 1990s, even with mainline carriers like Balkan Bulgarian. A total of 571 Il-18s were built at the Khodynka factory in downtown Moscow between 1957 and 1969, although various military variants followed later. Balkan's last Il-18s were not retired until 1998, 36 years after the first delivery to predecessor Tabso in 1962. LZ-BEA is seen at Sofia in September 1994, then one of six aircraft still in the fleet.

Balkan was also developing a taste for Western airliners, but remained a bastion for Soviet industry until the airline's bankruptcy in 2002. And what a fleet it had. In Soviet times, Balkan was the largest Tu-154 operator after Aeroflot, although the Chinese caught up in the early 1990s (a total of 36 Tu-154Ms went to China). In 1994, Balkan was still flying a mix of 24 Tu-154Bs, B-1s, B-2s and Ms, 22 years after the delivery of its first Tu-154. The original Tu-154 and -154As had faced fatigue problems with their lightweight wing structure, and were quickly superseded by the 'B' models with a redesigned wing and reinforced fuselage. The B-1 could be configured with up to 160 seats, and the B-2 with up to 180 seats. However, it was unusual to find any Tu-154s with more than 166 seats.

As with the Tu-134 (in 1968), Balkan held the prestigious distinction of being the first export customer for the -154. To deserve such an honour – twice – more than demonstrated that Bulgaria was consistently in Moscow's good books for many years. Interflug, LOT and others would surely have been very envious.

Balkan had long operated a remarkable network that seemed way out of proportion for the needs of Bulgaria's travelling population. In 1964, Il-18s inaugurated flights all the way to Lima, Peru, with stops in Africa on the way. Balkan never operated the Il-62, so the medium-haul Tu-154s also ventured far and wide. Occasionally, they would be seen on ad-hoc flights in Canada and the US. Other than regular Cubana Tu-154s in Montreal and Toronto, and rare visits to Miami by a lone Guyana Airways Tu-154M, the Tu-154 was almost unknown in North America. It was left to the Bulgarians to wave the Tupolev flag in cities like New York and Chicago. Tu-154M LZ-BTX is seen day-stopping in Nairobi in June 1992.

Balkan's last Tu-134As were retired by 1995. Part of the fleet is seen enjoying a restful time in Sofia in April 1994, although appearances are not what they seem. Only LZ-TUS is a genuine Balkan example, and the others were flown on government duties. LZ-TUU and -TUV, previously in service with the Czechoslovak government, both had spacious 47-seat VIP interiors. Just visible above -TUU's cockpit is a non-standard communications aerial, which you would not find on a regular airline -134. In total, 13 Tu-134s flew with Balkan, and another nine with the government.

Bulgaria was to have a long and fruitful association with Antonov turboprops, and in Balkan's case it would be with the An-12 and An-24. Here is 1969-vintage An-24B LZ-ANP, running up its Ivchenko AI-24 turboprops in Sofia. Balkan was still flying 14 An-24s on local and regional services in 1994, but had started to withdraw aircraft from service as they ran out of hours.

Soviet custom had always seen an aircraft's type written clearly and proudly on the forward fuselage, and the Bulgarians followed this tradition with great flair. Note the flowing 'Antonov 24' script under the flight deck windows. It didn't matter that the first An-24 flew as far back as 1959, and that LZ-ANP itself was already 25 years old; Balkan was happy to remind its passengers that they were privileged to be flying in a trusty An-24. This contrasts with the approach some airlines take today. If you walk around the outside of any British Airways Airbus or Boeing, there is nothing to tell you what kind of aircraft it is. You just have to try and guess.

Like Balkan, Romania's Tarom was a faithful An-24 and Il-18 operator. Il-18E YR-IMJ, seen landing at Athens' old Hellinikon Airport in August 1995, was then in its 28th year of service with the airline. Tarom also retired its last Il-18 in 1998, a full 37 years since the delivery of its very first example. The closest competitors to the Il-18, the Lockheed Electra and Vickers Vanguard, could not come close to matching the graceful Ilyushin's longevity with a single operator.

In 1994 Tarom was still flying four Il-18s, with another four stored in Bucharest. Although usually fitted out with up to 105 seats, the passenger interiors were often stripped out and the aircraft used as freighters (as in the case to Athens, where they would be loaded with thousands of cigars). As with other Soviet types like the Tu-134, the Il-18's miniscule passenger doors (only 1.4m high and 0.76m wide) appeared to have been designed for a submarine rather than for an aircraft. They were certainly not adapted for loading cargo. The frustrated cargo handlers in Athens must have been delighted when they heard that the dedicated Il-18GrM freighter YR-IMZ of sister airline Romavia was coming instead, boasting its large freight door. Romavia, closely affiliated to the Romanian government, operated two Il-18s. The other was YR-IMM, seen lining up in Athens in June 1996.

Among the Eastern Bloc airlines, there are many veteran executives who will say that the Il-18 was the greatest Soviet airliner ever built. It was rugged, reliable and easy to maintain. In the 'long range' Il-18D variant, it offered a range with maximum payload of close to 4,000km. This was substantially more than its replacement, the Tu-154, could offer in its early years. It would take the much-improved Tu-154M to rival the Ilyushin's range.

However, some passengers would be less inclined to praise the Il-18. While the seats were comfortable and there was lots of room, the roar of the Ivchenko AI-20 turboprops inside the cabin was something else – once measured at 118 decibels in the propeller plane on take-off. Hopefully the passengers on board YR-IML, departing from Zurich in May 1994, are enjoying the ride anyway.

Tarom's large fleet of An-24s, once numbering 31 aircraft, was winding down steadily in the early 1990s. Given the airline's limited domestic and regional markets, why did it need so many? It was even more remarkable that the airline also flew ten An-26 freighters. By 2004, just seven ATR turboprops were doing what the Antonovs had done before.

Unlike all its contemporaries in Eastern Europe, Tarom never operated the Tu-134. Romania had a long association with the BAC One-Eleven instead, which also involved the final assembly of nine aircraft in Bucharest. Tarom did fly 12 Tu-154Bs (see photograph on page 5) and five Il-62s (including two Il-62Ms), all of which were retired by 1997. However, back to the faithful Il-18: here is Romavia's Il-18GrM YR-IMZ, laden with cigars and leaving trails of cigar-like smoke as it departs Athens in May 1995.

The Eastern European airlines had all attained their biggest-ever fleets of Soviet-built aircraft by 1990, and so had Cubana. The big difference in the years to come lay in money and politics; LOT, CSA, Malev and others were all able to find financing or willing lessors to supply them with new Airbuses and Boeings, and nobody was stopping them. In faraway Havana, cash was short and the US government had a strict embargo in place that prevented the acquisition of Western-built aircraft.

So, just 367km from Miami (and 169km from Key West), the atmosphere at Havana's José Marti Airport was very different – and very special. In September 1991, one of Cubana's four Yak-42s heads a line-up of a single Tu-154B and three Il-62s. Apart from a leased DC-10 and an ageing Bristol Britannia just visible in the far distance, everything here at José Marti is Soviet-built, right down to the distinctive electric airstairs.

Cubana was then flying no fewer than 12 Il-62Ms, two Il-76s, five Tu-154B-2s, four Tu-154Ms and four Yak-42s. Fourteen Yak-40s and 12 An-24s flew domestic services. A further 16 An-26s flew in Cubana colours, but most (if not all) appeared to be operated by the military. The fleet sounded impressive, but utilisation was low. Erratic spares supply has plagued Cubana for decades. There was always a long line of aircraft waiting for action, or waiting for spares, on the far side at José Marti.

Cubana's Il-62s, usually configured for 158 passengers, had nevertheless been enjoying a little extra use with Cuba's growing popularity among European holidaymakers. Paris and Madrid had long been flagship destinations for the Ilyushins, but charter programmes also took the aircraft elsewhere, including Frankfurt and London (Gatwick). Canadians had long topped the list of visitors to Cuba, and in the winter of 1990–91 there were four Cubana flights each weekend to Toronto, and three to Montreal.

In Toronto you could sometimes buy a last-minute package for a week in Varadero, Holguin or Havana for just over 200 Canadian dollars, with everything included – including the excitement of flying there and back with Cubana in a Tu-154 or Il-62. Some wily Toronto residents would claim that it was cheaper to go to Cuba for a week than to stay at home.

Cubana's last four Il-62Ms were among the last off the line, and CU-T1280 was barely three years old when seen here on short finals to Toronto in February 1991. The embargo meant that Cubana had to stay with its elderly Soviet fleet much longer than its colleagues over in Eastern Europe. The Russians came to the rescue in 2005, when the first of three Il-96s arrived to relieve the long-serving -62s.

In 1991, Cubana still had four Il-18s on its books. After 22 years of passenger service, and despite its undersized doors, CU-T900 was operated as a freighter for at least three years (later as CU-C900, the 'C' for Carga) before being converted to full GrM freighter status for sister company Aero Caribbean, for which the aircraft served another seven years. Here is CU-T900 inbound to Toronto in August 1990.

We cannot leave Cuba without a few words on Aero Caribbean. Already famous as the world's last operator of the Bristol Britannia, the airline was also the last operator of the Ilyushin Il-14 in commercial service. Il-14M CU-T925, originally delivered to Cubana in 1957 and fitted out with 32 seats, was mainly used to fly vacation groups south from Havana to the small but growing resort of Cayo Largo. Three veteran Douglas DC-3s supported the old Ilyushin.

Aero Caribbean's marketing team clearly thought that Western visitors would adore the Il-14's 1950s decor and clattering Shvestov Ash-82T radial engines, but it was not quite the case. It also became difficult to source parts for the Il-14, as well as for the DC-3s. CU-T925 is seen running up its rattling Shvestovs at José Marti in September 1991. Not many Il-14s were fitted with a pointed black nose, which housed the Groza-40 weather radar. To their great credit, the Cubans kept this magnificent machine airworthy until 1999.

In the early 1990s, Aero Caribbean also flew four An-26s and two Yak-40s. The An-26s, like Cubana's examples, served Cayo Largo as well. While based on the An-24, with similar AI-24VT engines, the -26 had been designed in the 1960s as a purpose-built military transport aircraft.

Holidaymakers who might have complained about the Il-14 were no more enamoured with the An-26. They would board through the rear cargo door, find that there were hardly any windows and wonder why the cabin was fully equipped to drop paratroops. The trip to Cayo Largo in a gloomy, noisy cabin, shaking with the vibration of the Ivchenko turboprops thundering away outside, was certainly a new experience for many. CU-T112 is pictured in Cayo Largo in February 1991.

Across the Caribbean Sea, Nicaragua's Sandinista government had close ties with the Soviet Union. As with a few other countries around the world, Soviet influence and support often included supplying aircraft to the national airline, either on very attractive commercial terms, or in a barter agreement for something in exchange, or as a gift. It is thought that the two brand-new An-32 turboprops and a single Tu-154M 'ordered' by flag carrier Aeronica fell into the latter category. They were presented to Sandinista leader Daniel Ortega in 1989. An-32 YN-CBV *Zinica* is seen arriving in Managua after a discreet mission for the military in September 1991.

A taxiing An-32 coming straight at you is an intimidating sight. The big Ivchenko AI-20D engines are mounted high on the wings, and are an amazing 80% more powerful than those on the An-26 (the -32 shares the same fuselage). The large 4.7m diameter AV-68DM propellers had been designed especially for the -32 by the Soviet Union's propeller specialists, the Stoopino Machinery Design Bureau, outside Moscow. The engines, props and triple-slotted flaps were all brought together to give the burly Antonov exceptional performance from hot-and-high airfields, originally to meet the stringent requirements of the Indian Air Force.

Aeronica's colourful Tu-154M, YN-CBT *Momotombo*, did not fly often. In 1992, the aircraft was abandoned in Managua by the new incoming government. Five years later, it was rescued by an enterprising Russian repair team and flown back to Moscow.

Outside Europe and Cuba, there had been surprisingly few other Soviet airliner strongholds. The list would not surprise anyone following geopolitical developments from the 1960s onwards. The eclectic mix of countries included China, North Korea, Vietnam, Laos, Mali, Mongolia, Afghanistan, South Yemen, the Republic of Guinea and Syria. Aviaexport had succeeded in placing Yak-40s in West Germany and Italy, but otherwise the Western world preferred Western aircraft.

Syrianair had long run a professional operation with Caravelles, and then Boeing 727s and even 747SPs. The fleet planners in Damascus must have been taken by surprise when six Tu-134B-3s arrived between 1982 and 1984, and even more so when three Tu-154Ms arrived in 1985. Three of the -134s were in a VIP configuration for government use. The other three were fitted with 76 seats and saw limited airline service, but never really found their place across the network. The same held true for the -154s, which were delivered with 143 seats. Tu-154M YK-AIA is visiting Athens in June 1996.

It was a different story in Vietnam. Accustomed to flying Soviet-built airliners since the end of the Vietnam War, Vietnam Airlines (formerly Hàng Không Viêt Nam) was flying no fewer than 15 Tu-134s, 13 An-24s, nine Yak-40s and its last Il-18 on passenger schedules in 1991. As many as eight -134s could be scheduled to Bangkok from Hanoi and Ho Chi Minh City in a single day. Tu-134B-3 VN-A120 is seen in Bangkok in November 1991.

Chapter 2

All Change – a New Dawn

From 1992 onwards, these established operators of Soviet airliners continued on as usual. Their main objective appeared to be the introduction of Airbuses and Boeings as soon as possible. It was Aeroflot that would undergo the most radical change. In aviation terms, the fragmentation of the Soviet Union meant the fragmentation of Aeroflot and, therefore, the great Soviet fleet. There were incredible, unprecedented changes to come.

The new airlines in the new CIS were invited to take over whatever was sitting on the tarmac in Tashkent, Yerevan, Kiev and all the other old Aeroflot bases. In Russia, initially the Aeroflot regional directorates were encouraged to continue on as they had done before, but under a new identity and with the mandate to transition to new, financially independent companies as quickly as they could. Assets were often auctioned off or just taken over by new owners. The Russian government kept significant shareholdings in some of the new airlines, but sold them (or shut the airlines down) in the years to come.

Sometimes, the directorates would fragment themselves, as in Magadan, and their UADs would become independent entities in their own right. Chukotavia and its small fleet in Anadyr followed this trend. Perhaps on the wrong side of the tracks, there would be other new entities like 'Air Transport School', which quickly found lucrative work for its muscular, overpowered An-32 with the United Nations in Somalia. Seen arriving in Nairobi from Mogadishu in June 1992, CCCP-48057's crew was arrested as soon as the engines had shut down, and the aircraft was impounded. The *Kenya Times* later reported that the Antonov had flown to Mogadishu earlier in the day not with relief supplies but with a full cargo of banknotes, almost all Kenyan Shillings. The mission was not exactly what the UN had in mind.

There was a different story to be told at every Aeroflot outpost. Elsewhere in Siberia, and at the other end of the scale, the Tolmachovo United Air Detachment within the West Siberian Civil Aviation Directorate in Novosibirsk was renamed Sibir (Siberia Airlines). Sibir had an instant fleet of Il-86s, Tu-154s, An-24s and An-26s, along with an extensive hangar complex and more than enough well-trained personnel. Full of the entrepreneurial spirit in the new Russia, a young army officer called Vladislav Filev and his wife Natalia moved quickly and somehow bought the whole lot. Sibir is now S7, Russia's second biggest airline – and one of the few Russian airlines that made it through the boom years of the 1990s and survived.

While the long-established operators (Aeroflot included) all rushed after new Western equipment, there were countless start-ups that couldn't wait to get their hands on cheap Antonovs, Ilyushins, Tupolevs and Yaks. It was gold rush time in Russia, when suddenly almost anything was possible.

The challenges in transferring entire Aeroflot directorates over to their new owners in the CIS were not to be underestimated. Aircraft, hangars, training facilities, buildings, ground equipment – and thousands of personnel – now belonged to brand-new entities. In Armenia, for example, Aeroflot's Armenian Civil Aviation Directorate, which had included the 1st Yerevan United Air Detachment/113th Flight at Erebuni Airport and the 2nd Yerevan UAD/297th Flight at Zvartnots, became Armenian Airlines. The new airline, whatever its secret fleet preferences might be, was immediately equipped with a total of 32 jets: Yak-40s, Tu-134s, Tu-154s and even four Il-86s. A single An-32 and An-12 were thrown in for good measure.

As in the other CIS countries, there were mountains of bureaucracy to be overcome. New corporate identities would be introduced. Aircraft would have to be repainted and re-registered with new country prefixes. New individual agreements would have to be negotiated for international routes.

It was impossible to achieve all of this overnight. In a spirit of impressive pragmatism and cooperation, many of the new airlines continued to carry Aeroflot titles on their aircraft and fly with Soviet 'CCCP-' (SSSR- in English) registrations during 1992. Even the Soviet flag lived on for a few more months.

Armenian Airlines was soon flying its Il-86s on a prestigious new route to Paris. Wearing both its old Soviet registration and Aeroflot titles, CCCP-86118 is seen at Charles de Gaulle awaiting its return to Yerevan in October 1992.

Georgia was another new CIS country that was content to 'stay Soviet' for a while longer. ORBI Georgian Airways, which started out as Transair Georgia, was formed as the new (short-lived) national carrier in 1992. Its new fleet, transferred from Aeroflot's CAD in Tbilisi and Sukhumi, included 15 Tu-154B-2s, 14 Tu-134As and 12 Yak-40s. Tu-154B-2 CCCP-85496, showing off its temporary 'Aeroflot Georgia' colours, is arriving in Frankfurt from Tbilisi and Istanbul in June 1992.

Even the Ukrainians painted small Aeroflot titles on some of their aircraft, which would be unthinkable today. Urgently wanting to be up and running with a transatlantic operation, Air Ukraine negotiated a sweetheart deal for LOT's seven unwanted Il-62Ms, just days after the Soviet Union fell. Strangely enough, the massive fleet of Aeroflot aircraft inherited by Ukraine had not included any long-haul aircraft.

From early 1992 the aircraft flew under Soviet marks, with small Aeroflot titles. Il-62M CCCP-86133 is seen departing from Shannon for New York in October 1992, still in its hastily adapted LOT colours.

Air Ukraine wasted little time in starting the repainting process. There were a lot of aircraft to push into the paint shop. Aeroflot's huge Ukrainian CAD was thought to comprise as many as 15 flight detachments at different bases, operating close to 250 aircraft. This figure did not even include all the elderly An-2 biplanes scattered around the country, now under Air Ukraine's control.

UR-86134, one of the former LOT Il-62Ms, is seen landing in Shannon in December 1994. It has been re-registered with Ukraine's 'UR' prefix and repainted in perhaps the definitive Air Ukraine colours. The cautious 'perhaps' is because the rushed repainting process meant that all kinds of blues and yellows and fonts and title arrangements appeared across Air Ukraine's vast fleet. Any shade of blue or yellow paint that could be found in the paint shop would do.

Tu-134A UR-65761, one of 26 then in the fleet, is showing off a smart darker blue at Istanbul's Ataturk Airport in August 1995.

Air Ukraine was a big operator of Yakovlev trijets, inheriting some 18 120-seat Yak-42s and 24 32-seat Yak-40s from Aeroflot's Ukrainian Civil Aviation Directorate. It did not take long before many of the Yaks were dispersed to regional carriers in Ukraine, or even sold off to private owners. Yak-40 UR-87547, landing in Athens in April 1995, was being flown for Odessa-based Ironimpex.

Ukraine had a special association with the Tu-134, as the type was built in Kharkov, some 400km to the east of Kiev. The 852 aircraft from Kharkov's factory no. 135 were built between 1963 and 1984, although the last aircraft was not finally delivered until 1989. Despite being marked as a 'Tu-134A-3', UR-65718, seen visiting Heathrow in December 1993 in interim Air Ukraine colours, is a Tu-134AK with a VIP interior. This version can be identified from the additional passenger door on the port side, just in front of the engine. Some Tu-134AKs even had their own built-in airstairs at this position.

The Tu-134A's 6,800kg thrust Soloviev D-30-II engine has a similar designation to the big Solovievs on the Tu-154M, Il-62M and Il-76, but has (at the most) only 15% in common. The Tu-134A-3 and B-3 had slightly more powerful engines, the D-30-III. All these variants had cascade-type thrust reversers, unlike the very first Tu-134s, which had a breaking parachute for use on short or wet runways. It was apparently quite an unusual passenger experience when the parachute was deployed on the landing roll. Your seat belt (if there was one) might help keep you in your seat, but your head would likely collide with the seatback in front as the parachute popped out.

Of all the CIS countries outside Russia, Ukraine produced far more new airlines than anywhere else. The steady dispersal of Air Ukraine's fleet across the country resulted in a variety of new operators and colour schemes. Aeroflot had once based a United Air Detachment in Dnepropetrovsk, in Ukraine's southeast on the mighty Dnepr river. This, in turn, became a separate operating base for Air Ukraine, which later transitioned into a 'new' independent airline, Dniprovia. Others followed during the 1990s, including Donbassaero from Donetsk, Lviv Airlines and Odessa Airlines.

With plenty of available aircraft, low-cost manpower and lots of operational expertise, the Ukrainians were also adept at securing lucrative contracts overseas, including significant work for the United Nations. Yak-40 87918 was transiting through Athens in February 1993 after flying in Cameroun for Unitair.

In these early post-Soviet days, note that such minor details as a country prefix had not been added to the registration. The Yak could have come from anywhere and was probably breaking numerous ICAO rules with its lack of a national identity. It then flew locally for Dniprovia, and is seen resplendent in Athens again in July 1996.

Like the Tu-134, Antonov's twin turboprops have a strong Ukrainian legacy. Of an estimated 1,350 An-24s built, a thousand came off the production line in Svyatoshino, Kiev, between 1959 and 1977 (the rest were assembled in Russia, in Ulan Ude and Irkutsk). Three new Ukrainian airlines – Air Urga, Omega and Air Crimea – are showing off their smartly repainted An-24s in Istanbul in August 1995.

The Ukrainians certainly went wild when it came to the formidable Ilyushin Il-76 freighter. It did not take long before many former Soviet Air Force Il-76s suddenly found themselves with new civilian operators. It probably helped that the new Ukrainian Air Force, with at least 100 of the big capable Ilyushins on its hands in 1992, realised that the aircraft could earn valuable dollars in airline service.

Since its first flight in March 1971 from Khodynka in Moscow (where the first three aircraft were built), more than 800 Il-76s had been delivered in Soviet times from Factory 84 in Tashkent, Uzbekistan. The majority went to the military.

There are thought to be as many as 20 Ukrainian 'civilian' operators who flew military Il-76MDs (with military crews) in the 1990s. Many did not last more than a couple of years, including *Belbek 5P*. One of three aircraft in the fleet, well-worn UR-76580, is seen blasting away from Athens in May 1995. The MD variant is easily identified by its tail gunner's turret. This must have been an interesting, if lonely, place to experience a flight in an Il-76.

Khors Air was a much bigger entity, with 17 different Il-76MDs recorded over the short heyday when Ukrainian Il-76s were simply everywhere. UR-76664, its nose pointing purposefully towards the runway in the characteristic -76 approach profile, is coming into Athens in June 1996.

Two more Ukrainian 'wolves in sheep's clothing' are here together in Athens in March 1995. Busol Airline's Il-76 UR-76415 was marked simply as an 'Il-76' on the forward fuselage, but in fact this aircraft had seen service as an Il-78 tanker. The small pod housing the lights for aerial refuelling at night is visible just below the tail turret. Busol is the Ukrainian word for stork, and the airline featured its stork logo on the tail. Busol Airline's take on the Ukrainian national colours involved an unusually dark shade of yellow that was more like gold.

EcoPatrol's three Il-76MDs, seconded from the Ukraine Air Force's base in Zaporozhye, were supposedly flown on environmental duties for the government. The heavy, noisy and smoky Il-76 seemed an odd choice as a flagship for an environmental agency. The maximum take-off weight of the Il-76MD is 190 tonnes, which can include a maximum fuel load of 90 tonnes. Whenever an EcoPatrol Il-76 actually did go out on patrol (if ever), it would have been sure to leave a massive trail of CO_2 lingering in its wake.

The original Ilyushin 76 shared very similar engines to those on the Il-62M, the Soloviev D-30KP turbofan. The thrust rating was slightly higher for the Il-76, at 12,000kg compared to 11,000kg. With lots of power, two-section triple-slotted flaps and impressive leading-edge slats, there was no doubt that the Il-76 was designed for austere airfields with limited runways. Sixteen mainwheels and no fewer than four nosewheels were well adapted for rough surfaces. Given this capability, it would often come as a surprise to see how a fully laden Il-76 departed from a long 3,000m runway at a major airport. Even at maximum take-off power, it would appear to use almost every inch of the available concrete. The air would still be shaking minutes later.

The other new CIS countries were rather more restrained, particularly if their new governments found it hard to break from Soviet traditions. Uzbekistan, like Ukraine, had a great record in building aircraft. A total of 830 An-12s and now close to 900 Il-76s have been built in Tashkent, deep in the heart of central Asia.

However, the Uzbeks saw no need to allow a Ukrainian-style frenzy of start-up airlines or the slow break-up of their new airline, Uzbekistan Airways. The reverse was the case. Although it inherited more than 100 aircraft from Aeroflot's bases in Tashkent and Samarkand, Uzbekistan Airways had ambitious plans; however, it did not have the right aircraft.

Aeroflot's Uzbek CAD included ten impressive Il-86s, but Uzbekistan Airways was under pressure from the government to start high-profile routes to cities like London and even New York. The sector to London could take as long as seven hours depending on the prevailing winds, and was beyond marginal for the -86. Just as Air Ukraine was securing LOT's spare Il-62Ms, the Uzbeks moved fast and did the same with the redundant Interflug fleet.

A few months after the collapse of the Soviet Union, Uzbekistan Airways had the Il-62s ready to go, had negotiated route rights with the UK, and secured precious landing slots at Heathrow. The first-ever service between Tashkent and London was flown on 30th October 1992, not a bad achievement. UK-86579, which was also operated for the government, is seen in its new colours on finals to Heathrow in November the following year.

Along with the Il-86s, Uzbekistan Airways took over an impressive fleet of 21 Il-76, 22 Tu-154s, 23 An-24s, 25 Yak-40s and two An-12s. As with other Aeroflot directorates, the size of the fleet was out of all proportion to the actual network requirements for the aircraft. The new Uzbekistan team calculated that it only really needed a quarter of the aircraft it had been assigned. New Airbuses and Boeings would soon make most of this huge fleet redundant anyway, just like everywhere else. For good measure, Uzbekistan Airways even brought in BAe Avro RJ85s and the ungainly new Il-114 turboprop as well, locally produced in Tashkent.

The Yak-40s and An-24s had a busier time than the big Ilyushins and Tupolevs. Yak-40 UK-87457, by then 24 years old, is seen arriving at Fergana from Tashkent in June 1998. The little Yak seemed out of place at this huge, dusty airfield in the Fergana Valley, in the east of Uzbekistan. Fergana had been used by the Soviet military as a major base during their long war in nearby Afghanistan. In 1998 this wild place was still full of abandoned An-12s and assorted helicopters. Old habits die hard, and the Uzbek soldiers patrolling the airport were very unhappy that someone would dare to take a picture of the ageing Yak-40.

Uzbekistan's fleet came in different variations of several colour schemes. Tu-154M UK-85776, in Athens in July 1996, is wearing the standard livery of the time, which in turn would be replaced by the design that has continued to today. Originally destined to join Aeroflot's Uzbek Civil Aviation Directorate in 1993, this Tupolev was delivered straight to Uzbekistan Airways.

Il-62M UK-86573 visited Athens in November 1995. This was the oldest Il-62 in the fleet and had originally been delivered to Interflug in 1981. Not unlike Lufthansa, Interflug had always won high marks for its high maintenance standards and spotless aircraft. The Uzbek Il-62s were thought to be the best Il-62s out there.

Sister ship UK-86575, displaying its elegant lines and distinctive 'dog tooth' on the wing leading edge, is climbing out from the same airport just a month later.

Some of the old Soviet fleet began to adopt the smart new corporate colours, which featured blue on the top of the fuselage and green on the bottom – making a sort of giant Uzbek flag. Tu-154B-2 UK-85600, heading a line-up in Tashkent in June 1998, has a large flag on the tail rather than the airline logo, denoting it as a VIP aircraft flown for the government.

Around 670km away in Almaty (formerly Alma Ata), Kazakhstan, the Kazakhs had also taken over a monster fleet from Aeroflot. Aeroflot's Kazakh Civil Aviation Directorate had operated from 13 different bases in this vast country, the size of Western Europe. They left behind seven Il-86s, 26 Tu-154s, nine Tu-134s, four Il-76s, ten An-26s, nine An-30s, as many as 40 An-24s and over 30 Yak-40s.

The fleet initially went to newly formed Kazakhstan Airlines (Kazair). Somehow there was never the focus and vision (and government support) at the new national carrier in Almaty compared to their Uzbek neighbours. There was also no objection from the Kazakh government to new start-up airlines in the country. Kazakhstan Airlines survived five years before running out of money and being replaced by Air Kazakstan (no 'h'), which started flying in March 1997. By the early 2000s, Air Kazakstan was running into trouble as well.

Most of the Kazakhstan Airlines fleet, like this Tu-154B-2 UN-85781 at Heathrow in March 1994, and An-24 UN-46699 in Athens in December 1994 (just marked 'Kazair'), continued to wear the basic Aeroflot cheatline.

While Kazakhstan Airlines struggled to make its way in the 1990s, there was a steady stream of new Kazakh airlines that came and went, some lasting only a couple of years. SAN Air Company's Tu-154M RA-85825 looks very smart on the ramp in Athens in June 1997. Based in Karaganda, SAN was partly German-owned (hence the stylised flag just forward of the wing). SAN leased four Tu-154s from Samara Airlines and Bashkirian Airlines in Russia, all of which had previously flown with LOT.

Tu-154B production had started to transition over to the Tu-154M in 1983. In total, 606 of the earlier Kuznetsov-powered Tu-154s came off the production line in Samara (formerly Kuibyshev), 860km to the southeast of Moscow. The newer Tu-154M was a popular choice for many start-ups across the CIS. It could haul 160 passengers and their bags almost 4,000km, and was relatively efficient by Soviet standards. Compared to earlier Kuznetsov NK-8-2U-powered Tu-154Bs, the Tu-154M burned up to 25% less fuel per seat. It would also (just) meet the future Stage III noise limits in Europe, while the older Bs would come nowhere close. There were plenty of fairly new Tu-154Ms on the market, and they were not expensive.

Late-production Tu-154M UN-85744 was just two years old when it joined short-lived Azamat in 1994. Originally destined for Aeroflot's Kazakh CAD, it somehow bypassed Kazakhstan Airlines. It is seen taxiing out at Istanbul's Ataturk Airport in August 1995. This aircraft crashed at Moscow's Domodedovo Airport in December 2010, flying with South East Airlines (page 118).

In the Caucasus, Armenian Airlines never had the luxury of graduating to the Tu-154M. A mix of ten Tu-154Bs, B-1s and B-2s was inherited from Aeroflot's Armenian CAD, along with four Il-86s (see page 30), nine Tu-134As and nine Yak-40s. While the Yaks did not last long at the airline, the rest of the fleet stayed busy developing a new international network from Yerevan. Athens was a prime destination for the new airline. 1977-vintage Tu-134A-3 EK-65072 is seen on short finals in May 1995, and Tu-154B-2 EK-85566 at dusk in December 1994.

Like some of its contemporaries, Armenian Airlines soon decided it wanted to change its colours again. In their last few years of service, some of the old Soviet fleet looked very smart in the new corporate livery. Tu-134A-3 EK-65044 was already 20 years old when seen here in September 1996.

Despite the airline's lack of enthusiasm in keeping its Yaks in service, the type lived on with one of the few new start-ups in Armenia, Dvin Air. While primarily focused on cargo operations with An-12s, Dvin acquired a couple of ageing Yak-40s (one each from Russia and Moldova) for passenger charters. 1973-vintage EK-87662 is seen in Athens in April 1997. It would have taken the Yak at least four hours to fly here from Yerevan, and that assumes it had secured permission to overfly Turkey. UR-87421, operated by Ironimpex in Ukraine, is visible behind.

The straight-winged Yak has the distinction of being the slowest jet airliner ever built, with a typical cruise speed of 260 knots. Its big wing, triple-slotted flaps and sturdy landing gear means it can operate from rough 1,000m airstrips, and – to be fair – speed was never in the design criteria. The 1,500kg thrust Ivchenko AI-25 engines (1,750kg with the later AI-25T) may have been small, but they produced more than enough black smoke to compensate for their size.

As in Kazakhstan and Armenia, Georgia's fledgling airline industry went through troubled times and many changes. The Aeroflot Georgian CAD, with divisions in both Tbilisi and Sukhumi, transitioned into Transair Georgia and then ORBI Georgian Airways in 1992. Fifteen Tu-154B-2s, 14 Tu-134As and 12 Yak-40s came with the package. ORBI would not survive until the end of the 1990s, and all the -134s had gone by October 1997. Tu-134A-3 4L-65774, then 16 years of age, is heading out for take-off in Athens in September 1995.

Tu-134s had been assigned to all the Aeroflot directorates in the republics that became the 12 countries within the CIS, apart from Turkmenistan and Uzbekistan – although, not to be left out, the Uzbekistan Air Force later flew one aircraft on VIP missions. The three Baltic states, Estonia, Latvia and Lithuania (who did not join the CIS), also graduated into independence with Tu-134 fleets.

Latvia had a longer association with the Tu-134 than its neighbours. Twelve Tu-134B-3s were transferred across from Aeroflot's 280th Flight in Riga to Latavio, the new national airline. Two then went to Baltic International, which had the support of US investors. In 1996, the airline was restructured as Air Baltic and moved right away to a Western-built fleet. Baltic International's YL-LBK is arriving in Frankfurt from Riga in May 1994.

All was not lost for the Tu-134 in Latvia. LatCharter found a niche in the corporate market from 1996, and operated six of the Latvian Tu-134B-3s for a few more years. All of the aircraft were smartly painted in a variety of colours. YL-LBE, seen in Dublin in October 1995, did not finish its Latvian tour of duty until as late as 2003.

Both Estonia and Latvia also inherited small fleets of Tu-154B-2s, which did not last long with either Estonian Air or Latavio. However, a new airline, ELK Estonian (Eesti Lennu Kompanii), managed to appropriate three brand-new Tu-154Ms that were destined for Aeroflot's Tallinn directorate in 1992. One of them moved on to the newly formed Baltic Express Line in neighbouring Latvia the following year. Despite the menacing grey skies, YL-LAI looks resplendent taxiing in at Istanbul's old Ataturk Airport in August 1995. It is still in its original ELK colours.

Lithuanian Airlines did not waste any time in repainting around half of Aeroflot's Lithuanian CAD fleet (12 Yak-42s, nine Tu-134s, four An-24s and three An-26s) with a green cheatline, maybe to show there was no longer any connection to Soviet times. The green colours only lasted two years, and a new corporate image of red, white and grey was introduced in early 1994. Tu-134A LY-ABD is seen sporting the interim green colours in February 1994, during a fuel stop in Toulouse en route from the Canary Islands to Vilnius. The new airline's -134s only stayed in service for two more years.

Until 1992, the Yak-42 had been a rare sight in Western Europe. Aeroflot had mainly kept the aircraft confined to domestic routes, and the only export customers were China and Cuba. When Lithuanian Airlines opened up a new international network from Vilnius, its big Yaks started venturing far and wide. Airports like London's Gatwick and Heathrow welcomed their first-ever Yak-42s on scheduled services, not that these exotic visitors lasted very long. Yak-42D LY-AAU (opposite) is on finals to Heathrow in February 1994, showing off its impressive flap area. It was an unusual sight slotted in between all the Airbuses and Boeings. Enjoying its new adventures across Western Europe, the same Yak is seen in Toulouse the following month.

Like the Yak-42, Aeroflot's 700-plus An-24s had not ventured much out of the Soviet Union. Air Moldova, which emerged from Aeroflot's Moldavian CAD in Chisinau (Kishinev in Soviet times) soon sent its fleet of Antonovs further afield. 48-seat An-24RV ER-46685 is ready to depart Athens in April 1994 for the return flight to Chisinau, 1,100km and two-and-a-half hours away. The noise up close to the AI-24A turboprops and Tumansky RU19A-300 booster jet in the starboard nacelle (also doubling as the APU) was not to be underestimated.

Even the Moldavian CAD in Kishinev had been allocated 12 Tu-134s, eight Tu-154s and a mix of 15 An-24s, An-26s and An-32s. That was just for domestic flying. As with so many other directorates, it is thought that utilisation was very low in Soviet times. Air Moldova is a survivor and still around today. The airline later moved into Airbuses and Embraer jets and made do with eight aircraft (in total) for everything it needed to do – all international.

Turkmenistan Airlines is another survivor, but less modestly than Air Moldova. Aeroflot's Turkmen CAD left eight Il-76s, 12 Tu-154s, four Yak-42s, ten Yak-40s and 22 An-24s to the new regime in Ashkhabad. Turkmenistan Airlines soon embarked on a major fleet renewal programme with Boeing. It was reported

that all the Soviet-built types had to be grounded by 1999, by presidential decree. Nevertheless, with no obvious replacement the Il-76s kept going. Late in 2020 Il-76TD EZ-F427, now 27 years of age, was busy shuttling backwards and forwards to Dubai and Abu Dhabi. Sister ship EZ-F425, in the original Turkmenistan colours, is inbound to Athens in June 1994.

The Belarussians enjoyed a long association with the Tu-134, as the ARZ-407 overhaul plant at Loshitsa, outside Minsk, had been the prime centre of Tu-134 expertise throughout the aircraft's career. Many Tu-134As were converted to A-3 standard, with Soloviev D-30 Series III engines, at ARZ-407.

In 1992 Belavia (at first just 'Belarus') inherited 24 assorted Tu-154s, 19 Tu-134As, 18 An-24s, seven An-26s and eight Yak-40s from Aeroflot's Belarussian CAD. This fleet was radically downsized in the following years. Tu-134A CCCP-65149 is taxiing onto the runway at Shannon for its weekly flight back to Minsk in October 1992. It is still wearing its Soviet marks, with both Belarus and small Aeroflot titles. It is unlikely that the small population base of Shannon or nearby Limerick really justified a new service to Minsk. The flight was targeted more at Belarussians who could connect with Aeroflot's transatlantic services.

While Belavia moved steadily to a Boeing and Embraer fleet, it soldiered on with its Tu-154Ms longer than most, and was one of the very last operators of the -154 on scheduled services.

Unlike the Ukrainian Air Force, the Belarussian Air Force did not form numerous start-up airlines to earn hard currency with its fleet of 24 Il-76s. It just formed one: Trans Avia Export. Il-76MD EW-78801 is enjoying a layover in Athens in December 1995, along with an old friend from its Soviet military days, Air Service Ukraine's UR-76732. After a short spell enjoying civilian life, the Air Service Ilyushin (and its crew) went back to the Ukrainian Air Force.

Chapter 3

Back in Mother Russia

With hundreds of aircraft in Aeroflot's fleet now 'lost' in 14 different new countries, what had been going on in Mother Russia?

Well, more of the same. Prior to 1991, Aeroflot had 21 distinct directorates across Russia. All of these, apart from the Sheremetyevo operation in Moscow, would be sold off or otherwise acquired by new entities. Some would stay affiliated with Aeroflot for a while. It was decided (at the highest levels in the Kremlin) that Aeroflot at Sheremetyevo, firmly focused on international flying as 'Aeroflot Russian International Airlines' (ARIA), would be an ambassador for Russia and continue the great legacy of the Aeroflot brand. In fact the new ARIA team would dramatically improve the brand, and make Aeroflot a world-class airline for safety, on-board service and reliability.

The new, downsized Aeroflot had 103 aircraft at its disposal, a mix of Il-86s, Il-62s, Tu-154s and Tu-134s. In a surprising move, five new Airbus A310s had already been ordered by the old Aeroflot in late 1989, and the first would arrive in July 1992. This radical decision had been justified by the disappointing range of the Il-86, and Aeroflot's complete dependence on the much smaller Il-62 for most long-haul flying. Almost all of Aeroflot's transatlantic schedules had long involved a fuel stop in Shannon. While this had been great for Shannon, the new Aeroflot knew that offering its passengers old-fashioned fuel stops was no longer acceptable in the modern competitive landscape.

Aeroflot, like most of its counterparts in the CIS and Eastern Europe, would now start to build up significant Airbus and Boeing fleets. However, this would take a while – so the majority of Aeroflot's passengers in the 1990s were still going to enjoy the noise, smoke and distinctive ambiance of the great Soviet airliners. Il-86 RA-86110 is turning on to the runway after refuelling in Shannon at dawn in March 1994 (opposite).

Shannon had played a huge role in Aeroflot's transatlantic operations since 1975. The tradition was to continue in the early days of ARIA in the 1990s. As the Shannon connection was originally linked solely to the limited range capability of the Il-62 and Il-86, it is worth a quick look at this great partnership with Aeroflot and Soviet aviation. With the slow demise of the classic Soviet airliner, Shannon would lose its most valuable customer after Aer Lingus.

Until the advent of the Il-96, Soviet long-haul types (excluding the immense Tu-114 turboprop) had always suffered from a range shortfall across the North Atlantic. Despite its four engines and impressive girth, the Il-86 widebody was not really a long-haul aircraft at all, and at best a six-hour aircraft that was better suited to European routes.

The Il-62, and in particular the Il-62M, were much more capable than the Il-86 but could not fly non-stop with a viable payload on Aeroflot's flagship route from Moscow to Havana. If there were adverse winter winds, an Il-62M could not even carry a full passenger load from Moscow to New York.

Gander had long been a favoured refuelling stop in Soviet times, but from September 1975 Aeroflot's Il-62s started calling in at Shannon as well. Knowing that Gander and Prestwick would be keen to win as much of Aeroflot's growing transit business as they could, the enterprising marketing team in Shannon went all out to ensure they would win everything.

By 1980, Aer Rianta (the Irish Airports Authority) had arranged for Aeroflot to have its own low-cost fuel supply in Shannon, brought in by sea from the Soviet Union. Three years later, this fuel was made

available for any aircraft transiting through Shannon. In the winter months, Aeroflot became the largest operator at the airport, carrying more passengers through Shannon than Aer Lingus. Here is Il-62M RA-86510, now proudly displaying the Russian flag, taxiing onto the runway during one of Shannon's frequent downpours in March 1994.

As the partnership expanded, in August 1988 Aer Rianta opened a new cabin refurbishing and paint hangar specifically for Soviet-built aircraft, sized to handle all Aeroflot's aircraft up to the Il-86. Nobody then would have envisaged that just six years later, in March 1994, the hangar would welcome aircraft like Pakistan's Hajvairy Air Il-86 RA-86113, not that this aircraft had a long career in Pakistan.

With the collapse of the Soviet Union, Aeroflot was now setting its sights on more US and South American destinations. All this was good news for Shannon. In August 1991, Aer Rianta and Aeroflot announced the construction of a purpose-built facility that could house up to 200 overnighting crew members. By the summer of 1992, Aeroflot's services from Moscow to Chicago, Miami, New York, Washington and Havana were all transiting through Shannon. Some of the Miami and Havana flights continued into Latin America, to destinations including Mexico City, Lima and Santiago.

While the stop in Shannon enabled the Il-62M to cope routinely with the longer transatlantic sectors westbound, it was far from the case with the range-challenged Il-86. The lumbering -86 would make a further fuel stop in Gander, the crew doubtless keeping a steady eye on the fuel gauges when faced with strong headwinds in the winter. Waking up everyone within a 20km radius of the airport and using up most of Shannon's 3,200m runway, RA-86067 is powering off for Gander in May 1993.

Aeroflot won fifth-freedom flights from Shannon for many of the services to the US, so became well known to the Irish population as the airline of choice (in fact the only scheduled airline at the time) to cities like Miami and Washington. In 1993, Irish holidaymakers could even travel to Barbados in the comfort of an Il-62. In 1993, no fewer than 2,300 Aeroflot flights passed through Shannon, an average of over six every day. The following year brought an additional bonus, with newly formed Air Ukraine's Il-62Ms stopping for fuel on the way from Kiev to New York and Toronto.

Shannon is not a busy airport, and in the early 1990s the locals would never have predicted that their peaceful, bucolic County Clare countryside would reverberate to the crackling roar of Kuznetsov and Soloviev turbofans several times a day.

While the ARIA team in Sheremetyevo was working on a new network strategy and negotiating for the latest Western equipment, new airlines were taking shape in almost every other city (and airport) in the country. This was great news for the rest of the Aeroflot fleet. In 1992, excluding ARIA's 100 aircraft, there were almost 3,000 assorted Antonovs, Ilyushins, Tupolevs and Yaks that were now going to be dispersed among close to 400 new airlines in Russia and the CIS over the next ten years. And these were just passenger aircraft. There were plenty of freighters available as well, often from the military.

The vast majority of these airlines did not last long. Some survived for just a matter of weeks, However, they all combined to breathe new life and energy, and much more utilisation, into their newly acquired aircraft.

There were also new markets to be explored. Russians were now free to travel abroad. Destinations like Greece, Cyprus, Turkey and Egypt were all easily accessible, and what better aircraft to take them there than the Il-86? These 350-seat leviathans were cheap (if not free); fuel was comparatively inexpensive, and there were no marginal transatlantic crossings.

Within Russia, the old Aeroflot had assigned Il-86s to its directorates in Novosibirsk, St Petersburg and Krasnoyarsk and to both the Vnukovo and Sheremetyevo bases in Moscow. No fewer than 22 Il-86s were absorbed into the new Vnukovo Airlines, alongside a similar number of Tu-154s. Athens became a big Vnukovo destination for Russian shoppers and holidaymakers, and Il-86 RA-86085 is seen climbing away in its racy new colours in August 1995.

To the south of Moscow, the Domodedovo Civil Aviation Production Association, previously part of Aeroflot's Moscow Territorial CAD, was also expanding beyond its traditional long-haul routes to Russia's Far East. No fewer than 40 Il-62s were transferred over to the new company, and three new Il-96s were to follow. For three years, the Domodedovo CAPA also operated three ageing Il-18s. These were among the last Il-18s to fly passengers in Russia. Il-18D RA-75462, at Istanbul in August 1995, was still in the high-visibility 'polar' colours it wore in its previous life as an Il-18DORR fisheries reconnaissance aircraft. Manufactured in 1967, it was one of only two Il-18s to have enjoyed this specialised role of policing the oceans around the Soviet Union and beyond.

While younger than the Il-18, this Il-62 also qualified for vintage status. Krasnoyarsk, far away in Siberia, had been another major Aeroflot stronghold, with 17 Tu-154s, four Il-86s and two Il-62s among several smaller types that were taken up by Kras Air. The Krasnoyarsk Region, or Eastern Siberian Federal District, is twice the size of Western Europe – quite impressive for a 'district'. The airline was among the last operators of the original, first-generation Kuznetsov-powered Il-62. RA-86708, taxiing out in Istanbul in August 1995, had been delivered new 21 years previously to LOT.

Like the Il-62, the Tu-154 programme had been revitalised by the move from fuel-thirsty Kuznetsov NK-8 engines to the more efficient Soloviev D30KU turbofans. Tu-154M RA-85747 displays its clean lines as it climbs away from Athens in August 1995. Although in Aeroflot colours, this aircraft was flying for ALAK, a short-lived charter operator based at Moscow's Vnukovo Airport.

Given that all 1,026 Tu-154s were built in Samara, 860km to the southeast of Moscow, it was logical that Samara Airlines, which emerged from Aeroflot's Volga CAD, would remain a loyal Tu-154 operator. It operated Tu-154Bs alongside Tu-154Ms right through the 1990s. Tu-154B-2 RA-85472, still with its Aeroflot cheatline, is taxiing out in Istanbul in August 1995.

There were several busy hotspots for Soviet aviation in the mid-1990s, with Sharjah certainly the most exotic. However, in terms of daily movements anywhere outside Moscow, nowhere could beat the old Ataturk Airport in Istanbul. A few years later there would be a long line of Turkish Airlines aircraft occupying every gate, but in 1995 there was lots of room for aircraft from Russia and almost every other CIS country.

All the visitors would be in and out within a couple of hours or less, usually in the late morning and early afternoon. The howl of Soviet jet engines, and high-intensity roar of Ivchenko turboprops, would be constant. There would always be something on the move.

In a frenzy of quick turnarounds, passengers and their baggage would be loaded in all kinds of interesting ways. The 'baggage', most of it merchandise from the great bazaars of Istanbul, would be sold again wherever it was headed. There could be as many as 20 large bundles per passenger. With the underfloor holds full, and cabins maybe not loaded in full accordance with ICAO regulations, some of the bundles might even be squeezed through the emergency exits of an Ilyushin or Tupolev.

Kazan, in Russia's autonomous Republic of Tatarstan, could alone merit four Tatarstan Airlines flights a day from Istanbul. Here, at the same time in August 1995, is Yak-42 RA-42333 surrounded by two Tu-134s, and 1981-vintage Tu-154B-2 RA-85488 taxiing out. The Tu-154 had seen service with the Czechoslovak government and then Czech charter airline Ensor Air, and it is still wearing Ensor's basic colours.

The Russians and Ukrainians were also busy in Istanbul with attractive lease proposals for Turkey's myriad of start-up airlines. Vnukovo Airlines had provided three Tu-154Ms and crews to Greenair as early as 1990, followed by a short lease of a 350-seat Il-86 (page 13). Greenair also brought in two Tu-134As as well, flown on its behalf by Russia's government flight. The 164-seat Tu-154s went back to Vnukovo Airlines in 1995, but no sooner had they been repainted in Vnukovo's colours they were back in Turkey again, now with Active Air. TC-ACI and TC-ACT are seen looking rather inactive in Istanbul in August 1995. Active Air lasted a matter of months, and the -154s were back in Russia by the end of the year.

Other short-lived newcomers included Holiday Air and Top Air, both of whom enjoyed a few months of Yak-42 operations. The early-production Holiday Yak-42 UR-42540 also arrived in Turkey in the spring of 1995, with a Tu-154M arriving later. The Top Air Yak-42D TC-IYI survived in the country until the following year.

Turkey's brief association with Soviet-built aircraft also extended to freighters. Both the impressively named Global Air Cargo and Avia Cargo System operated An-26s in 1995. TC-GZT and TC-ACS are seen awaiting some action that summer.

The hugely successful An-26 flew for the first time in May 1969, and just over 1,400 were believed to have been built in the Svyatoshino factory in Kiev before the last one was delivered in 1986. While most were delivered to the military in the Soviet Union and other air forces around the world, over 100 ended up with civilian operators – usually as the An-26B.

The An-26's 2,820ehp Ivchenko AI-24VT engines provide 10% more power than the AI-24As in an An-24RV, but short-field and hot-and-high performance capability have never been the strongest points of the -26, hence the development of the overpowered An-32 (page 27). The normal maximum payload for the An-26 would be 5.5 tonnes, compared to 7.5 tonnes for the brawny An-32. Perhaps the most striking and innovative feature on the An-26 is the rear loading ramp. It can either be used as exactly that, a ramp for vehicles or troops – or it slides unobtrusively forward under the fuselage, meaning trucks can back right up to the cargo hold.

CAT Cargo's An-12 TC-KET lasted in commercial service from 1994 to 1997, and has since languished at Ataturk Airport to this day.

Following the reunification of Germany and the collapse of the Soviet Union, the early 1990s also saw the break-up of Yugoslavia. After years of conflict (and more to come), newly formed nations like Macedonia and Bosnia-Herzegovina needed help to create new transport infrastructure and airlines. Sanctions against the once-Yugoslav (now Serbian) airline JAT prohibited the airline from operating in these new countries for several years.

As in Turkey, there were willing Russians and Ukrainians to help. In the Republic of Macedonia (also referred to as North Macedonia), Balkan Bulgarian was also involved from 1991, launching services for Palair Macedonian from Skopje and Ohrid, with two older Tu-154Bs. Tu-154B-1 LZ-BTJ was back in Sofia in April 1994, having been displaced at Palair by Fokker jets. This old Tupolev is still intact today, but you have to go underwater to inspect it. It was sunk in the Black Sea to become an artificial reef.

Yak-42s found favour in both Bosnia and North Macedonia, which brought more of the elusive Yaks into Western European skies. Flown by ex-Aeroflot crews, Bosna Air's RA-42385 'Skopje' arrives in Zurich in March 1993. Bosna Air became Vadar Bosna Air in 1993 and then disappeared. There were at least 12 Macedonian start-up airlines during the 1990s, including Avioimpex. Yak-42D RA-42389 is in Zurich in August 1993. Three months later sister ship RA-42390, also flying for Avioimpex, flew into Mount Trojani, near Ohrid, with the loss of all 115 on board.

Air Bosna lasted for much longer. In basic Air Ukraine colours and flown by Air Ukraine pilots, Yak-42D T9-ABD starts its leisurely climb-out from Dusseldorf in September 1999.

First flown in March 1975, the big Yak was a sedate performer. Its three 6,500kg thrust Lotarev D-36 engines delivered a cruise speed of less than 400 knots. The range of the first Yak-42s was poor (particularly in the context of the size of Russia), little more than 1,000km with a full payload. After building 63 -42s, Yakovlev introduced the more capable -42D. It could fly twice as far, and the economics were relatively good. It offered three tonnes of extra take-off weight and additional fuel capacity.

The Yak-42 was envisaged as a replacement for the Il-18 at Aeroflot and with the Soviet Union's captive airlines abroad. It was also hoped that the -42 was to be a Tu-134 replacement, but this was never going to make much sense: the passenger capacity of the -42 was 50% greater than that of the -134. There were plans for at least 1,000 to be built. Finally only 183 came off the production lines in Smolensk (just 11 aircraft) and then Saratov, often at a very slow rate, until the last aircraft was delivered in 2003.

Development issues with both the wing and new three-shaft Lotarev turbofan delayed service entry with Aeroflot until the end of 1980. There were further design problems with the tail and horizontal stabiliser. In June 1982, the stabiliser jackscrew failed on an Aeroflot Yak-42 en route from Leningrad to Kiev, and the aircraft fell out of the sky over Belarus. It was the first, and worst-ever, Yak-42 accident, with 132 killed. The type was grounded until late 1984 while numerous design modifications were implemented. The damage to the -42's reputation was huge, and this tragedy would not be forgotten in a hurry.

Thirty-eight years after this accident (in November 2020), and without hesitation, Konstantin Tereschenko, the commander of Rossiya's Special Flight Detachment (the government VIP flight) explained why the Yak-42 is the one Soviet airliner that has never served on VIP duties: 'The State commission (that was accepting the type for its ability to operate within the Brigade) was of the opinion that this aircraft was not safe. Specifically, this decision was based on the accident of the Yak-42 that took place in 1982 near Norvlya (Belarus).'

Fortunately, the Yak-42 was deemed safe after the lengthy redesign process. But the damage was done.

While Balkan Bulgarian was busy in Macedonia and elsewhere, a group of private investors had set up a new Bulgarian airline, Varna International Airways (known as Air VIA, or just VIA) as early as 1990. With plenty of good Tupolev expertise in Bulgaria, and a remarkably good deal for new aircraft, they bought five 166-seat Tu-154Ms. A sixth followed later. LZ-MIK, in the airline's definitive colours, is awaiting business in Sofia in April 1994.

While Air VIA focused on the European holiday market, it also chartered out aircraft elsewhere. LZ-MIR, the next aircraft in line, was ready to leave for a five-month assignment with Raji Airlines in Pakistan. Interestingly, every one of these five aircraft has a different presentation of the VIA titles.

VIA's Tupolevs were a regular sight around Europe for almost 15 years, when they were replaced by A320s.

Hemus Air was another long-time player in Bulgaria. From 1972 onwards 12 Yak-40s had served with Balkan, but they never quite found the right place in the fleet. As a big An-24 operator, Balkan soon realised that its 27-seat Yaks burned even more fuel than the 48-seat Antonov – and didn't really go any faster. In 1986, eight Yak-40s were transferred to a new subsidiary that was to focus on general utility and charter operations, Hemus Air. LZ-DOF is seen parked in Sofia in April 1994.

Over the years, Hemus expanded with Tu-134s and Tu-154s that were also handed down from the Balkan fleet. The airline was privatised in 2002 when Balkan went bankrupt. Turning full circle, four years later, Hemus became the major shareholder in Bulgaria Air, Balkan's successor.

The Yak-40s were configured either with a spacious 16-seat layout, 27 seats or 32 seats. In the 1990s Hemus operated extensively for other airlines, including Albania's Ada Air, and could thus offer lots of flexibility with configurations. LZ-DOM was flying Ada Air's schedule from Tirana to Athens in April 1996.

A rather different Bulgarian start-up took to the skies in November 1993, with all kinds of German connections. Air Zory had sourced a 100-seat Il-18 from Russia and flew this for four months before taking delivery of an Il-18GrM freighter (one of only two at the time) from Germany. The 'new' freighter, LZ-AZZ, is seen making a smoky approach to Athens in June 1994 (opposite).

The freighter conversion of the Il-18 came late in its life. In the 1980s, Interflug, Tarom, Balkan and Cubana had pushed Ilyushin hard for a full-freighter conversion programme, complete with a large cargo door. They all had Il-18s with plenty of remaining airframe hours that were no longer required as front-line passenger aircraft. However the Ilyushin design bureau seemed to have other priorities, and was disinclined to leap into action.

Things changed from 1992, when the lure of dollars and a new commercial world focused Ilyushin to look at the project again. It was encouraged by an old Interflug team that had been involved in winding up its once-great airline. The team had been involved with Interflug's Liquidation Committee, and had sold off the Il-62Ms to Uzbekistan and many Tu-134s back to Russia. Together with some experienced Il-18 pilots, they also created an airline called Berline, with five old Interflug Il-18s.

Berline's new management paid a nominal one Deutschmark for each Il-18, in lieu of the compensation package they were due when Interflug was shut down. Their intent was to fly passenger charters with the Il-18s but convert them later to freighters. Taking fortunate Germans on holiday, D-AOAO is taxiing in Athens in August 1993. In the early 1990s, it is unlikely that many passengers expected to be flying on a propeller-driven aircraft all the way to the eastern Mediterranean.

The ex-Interflug team, with lots of good contacts in Moscow, ferried another Il-18, D-AOAS, to the Ilyushin complex at Moscow's secret Zhukovsky airfield in September 1992. Five months later it reappeared as the first-ever GrM freighter. Berline experienced financial challenges in the winter of 1993–94, and hence the sale of two Il-18s to Air Zory.

In April 1994, Air Zory (named after founder Angel Karamihov's daughter Zorniza, or 'Zory') won a contract to operate a Lufthansa Cargo service from Frankfurt to East Midlands in the UK, five days a week. In June, Lufthansa reassigned the Il-18 to the Athens–Cologne route. The old Ilyushin's 3.5m by 1.8m door, 12,100kg payload and ability to carry three LD9 containers, or six LD3s, was highly attractive to Lufthansa.

In their very early days, Interflug's Il-18s flew in 'Deutsche Lufthansa' colours until 1963, despite repeated objections from the other Deutsche Lufthansa in West Germany. Over 30 years later, an Il-18 was again proudly wearing Lufthansa titles – but in a very different world. LZ-AZZ is seen taking on its Cologne-bound cargo in Athens in June 1994.

Chapter 4
The New Millennium

The gold rush of the 1990s was not to last long. The established flag carriers in Eastern Europe either transitioned to Western aircraft, or simply went bankrupt, like Balkan and Malev. More than half of the new airlines in Russia and the CIS disappeared, and many more would follow. Even most of the mysterious Ukrainian airlines operating military Il-76s vanished, almost as quickly as they had arrived.

Unfortunately, from 2000 onwards, the number of old airworthy Ilyushins and Tupolevs would start to see a rapid decline. There were several factors to hasten the demise of the great Soviet fleet.

Noise was one. Unless they had a special military or humanitarian reason to be there, all Il-86s, first-generation Il-76s, Il-62s, Tu-134s and earlier Tu-154s were banned from regular operation in many countries in the world from April 2002. The slightly quieter Tu-154M sneaked into the new Stage III category, but only just. It was ironic that the Il-86 had finally found its sweet spot as a 350-seat people-mover taking Russians to tourist resorts, only to be swiftly banned from flying to countries like Greece and Cyprus. In 2000, it was estimated that 40% of all Russians flying away on holiday would travel by Il-86.

Meanwhile, an ever-increasing number of comparatively modern Western jet airliners were available at competitive rates. The prodigious output of new A320 family aircraft and 'Next Generation' 737s released many earlier A320s and 737s on to the market. The 737-300 and -500 in particular became popular in the CIS. A 737-300 with 149 seats would burn slightly less fuel than a 76-seat Tu-134. Its CFM56 engines would stay on the aircraft at least four times longer before overhaul. The economics were very compelling.

Market forces had also not helped with the maintenance and overhaul of old Soviet airliners. The long-established overhaul shops in specialised centres like Minsk (Tu-134) and Moscow-Vnukovo (Tu-154) could charge whatever they wanted. Tu-134s were subjected to a substantial teardown every 6,000 hours, and the cost in Minsk was reported to have tripled – to around $500,000 – by 2000. That was often more than the value of the aircraft itself. What's more, you couldn't even fly your noisy -134 to cities like Athens any more.

Russia itself was certainly not constrained by new noise legislation. On the positive side, Aeroflot would continue to fly Tu-134s and Tu-154s for a few more years. A small number of Il-86s would stay busy with holiday traffic to Sochi and Simferopol on the Black Sea, and to Turkey and Egypt. Despite the demise of Balkan, Bulgaria could rightly claim to be a 'centre of excellence' when it came to An-12 operations in the new millennium, with new operators taking over where Balkan had left off. Various old Antonov freighters ended up just about everywhere, including the US, so there was still some new action to come.

Balkan Bulgarian stopped flying in 2002, but its five An-12s (and crews) were soon employed elsewhere. No fewer than seven other Bulgarian airlines were operating the versatile old Antonovs: Air Sofia, Bright Air Services, Bulgaria Flying Cargo, Heli Air Services, Inter Trans Air, Rila Air and Vega Airlines.

Vega operated six An-12s alone, and its smart LZ-VEA is seen visiting Toulouse in October 2001, no less than 40 years after it came off the production line in Tashkent. It is thought that 1,242 An-12s were manufactured in total between 1957 and 1972, of which only 183 were built for export. The vast majority went straight to the Soviet military. Other than Tashkent, early An-12s were also built in Irkutsk and Voronezh.

The new Stage III noise rules were obviously a catastrophic development for many airlines. Somehow the An-12 – one of the noisiest and smokiest turboprops out there – was qualified as Stage III compliant. Vega did not hesitate to boast about its 'quiet' old aircraft, later writing 'Chapter 3' on the side of each Ivchenko AI-20M engine, as seen on LZ-VEE in April 2005. Deafened ground crews must have been astonished to see such a claim as they marshalled the aircraft into its parking position.

Bright Air Services flew four An-12s. LZ-BRP visited Toulouse in April 2005. Despite the legend 'The Future is Bright' on the fuselage, the future was sadly less than bright. Bulgaria would join the European Union in January 2007, which meant that aircraft registered in the country would have to meet EASA certification rules. The An-12 had certainly never been certified to these rigid requirements, and it would be a huge and costly exercise even to attempt such a project. The old Antonov's career in Bulgaria came to an abrupt end. However, this did not stop several aircraft, and lots of experienced Bulgarian crews, moving quietly over to Ukraine – where there were no irritating details like EASA certification to worry about.

While the Bulgarian Antonov fleet was well known and well documented, it was starting to be a challenge to keep up with all the movements and changing fortunes of other An-12s. Well situated for flying interesting cargoes to countries like Afghanistan and Somalia, Sharjah, Fujairah and Ras-al-Khaimah in the United Arab Emirates became notorious for hosting many An-12s and all kinds of other Soviet aircraft as well. Teams of Russians and Ukrainians were on site to support them. Their flexible approach to operating procedures, and

a readiness to haul anything anywhere, gave a new lease of life to many An-12s and Il-76s, and also passenger aircraft. New operators came and went, sporting a variety of exotic colour schemes.

Aircraft ownership and certification details were often murky. Registrations could be changed overnight. The Republic of Guinea, Equatorial Guinea, Liberia, Sao Tomé, Sierra Leone and the Central African Republic were among the popular countries for registering, and re-registering, the old freighters. It was not evident whether the authorities in faraway Sierra Leone even knew that more aircraft had been added to their register.

In Southeast Asia, Phnom Penh in Cambodia also emerged as a popular staging post for itinerant Antonovs. In a familiar scene that would doubtless be repeated soon, this An-12 is about to be painted '3X-GIM' in Phnom Penh in June 2004. Supervised by two Russians, a local team is covering some of the rear fuselage with masking tape and old newspapers to ensure a good, clean result. '3X' is the registration prefix for the Republic of Guinea. However there was little sign of any representative from the Republic of Guinea's airworthiness offices in Conakry, almost 13,000km away.

For a short while, a Russian management team also operated up to five An-12s that were based in Phnom Penh (and registered in Cambodia), under the names Imtrec Aviation and Air People Company. XU-315, already 42 years old, is enjoying a quiet day in Phnom Penh in June 2004.

Various An-24s also moved to Cambodia with Russian and Ukrainian crews, including An-24B XU-335, displaying a cloudscape on the tail that the real clouds were doing their best to match. This 35-year-old veteran, parked at Siem Reap in June 2004, was one of two operated by Russian-owned Progress Multitrade Air (PMT Air) for Cambodia's President Airlines on domestic schedules and to Hanoi, Vietnam.

President Airlines competed vigorously with its ageing 48-seat Antonovs in the busy market from Phnom Penh to Siem Reap against brand-new ATR-72s of Siem Reap Airways. With President's fares a few dollars less, passengers would happily accept the unrestrained roar of Ivchenko turboprops close to their ears and forego the more refined comforts of the ATR-72.

President lasted for eight years (1997 to 2005), which was longer than many other Cambodian airlines. Royal Phnom Penh Airlines started up in 2002 but survived less than two years. Its Soviet airliners were in fact three Chinese-built An-24s, Yunshuji Yun-7-100Cs. The Chinese had secured an agreement to build An-24s under licence in 1966, but the programme was very slow to build up steam. The first delivery to CAAC did not take place until 1980. The Y-7-100 was a "modernised" version with winglets, which appeared in 1984. There were unkind reports that the fancy winglets actually worsened the An-24's performance, rather than improved it. All three of Royal Phnom Penh's Y-7s were awaiting a new future in Phnom Penh in June 2004.

The An-24 was proving more resilient elsewhere. SCAT, based in Shymkent in Kazakhstan, was formed in 1997. The airline has operated around 25 different An-24s since then, either with 46, 48 or 50 seats, and several are still going strong in 2021. An-24RV UN-47258 is taxiing out at Almaty in October 2006, with Il-76TD UN-73674 parked in the background.

The Kazakhs later introduced a novel registration system based on the aircraft type, so this particular An-24 became UP-AN419 – the 19th 'AN4' on the register. The 'UN' prefix was also changed to 'UP'. With a growing fleet of Western jets, SCAT decided to disassociate the hard-working old An-24s from its shiny jet fleet, so a subsidiary called Southern Sky was created specifically for the Antonov operation.

A quick diversion away from Antonov turboprops to Enimex's An-72 ES-NOG, landing at Arlanda Airport, Stockholm in March 2000. This very distinctive Antonov design emerged in the early 1970s as a future replacement for the An-26 in military service, and flew for the first time in August 1977. Its two Lotarev D-36 turbofans, the same as those on the Yak-42, were positioned high and forward of the wing. The exhaust would then blow over the top of the wing, creating significant extra lift (the 'Coanda' effect, named after a Romanian engineer).

Despite its ten-tonne payload and impressive airfield performance, the complex An-72 and very similar An-74 were just 'too much aircraft' to replace the simple, rugged An-26. Around 200 were built, the first few in Kiev and the rest in Kharkov. One of the few commercial An-72 operators, Enimex, based in Tallinn, Estonia, had seven aircraft. Most had seen service with the Soviet and then Russian military.

For sheer longevity, the robust An-12 and An-24 have broken all kinds of records, as we will see later. Their much larger big brother, the An-22, has not done badly either. At the time of writing, Antonov Airlines' famous UR-09307 – well followed wherever it goes – is still in service.

In June 1965, just four months after its first flight, the awesome (but then top secret) An-22 made a surprise appearance at Le Bourget for the Paris Airshow. With its wingspan of 64 metres, length of 57 metres and a maximum take-off weight of 225 tonnes, it was then the biggest aircraft in the world. Its dramatic, unexpected arrival certainly caught the attention of the world's press.

Although the usual maximum payload of the An-22 is 80 tonnes, in October 1967 the third development aircraft flew a payload of just over 100 tonnes to an altitude of 25,000 feet. The empty weight of the smaller An-12 before adding fuel and payload is 37 tonnes, so that feat was equivalent to carrying almost three An-12s at once. Given that the An-12 is considered a hefty machine in its own right, the An-22 puts heftiness in a new league.

The An-22 is powered by four Kuznetsov NK-12MA engines, at 15,000ehp the most powerful turboprops ever built. The huge AV-90 contra-rotating propellers, with a diameter of 6.2 metres, were designed and built by the Stoopino Machinery Design Bureau. Stoopino were the true propeller experts in Soviet times and (as with the An-32 earlier) had manufactured the propellers for most of the other Soviet turboprop designs.

Combined, the thunderous engines and contra-rotating props produce a noise like nothing else. Imagine a sort of agricultural threshing machine backed up by the roar of a giant furnace, and that is the An-22 up close.

Sixty-eight An-22s are thought to have been built between 1964 and 1976, two prototypes in Kiev and the rest in Tashkent. All production aircraft went to the Soviet military. However, in 1994 the Antonov Design Bureau at Kiev's Gostomel Airport never got around to giving CCCP-09307 back to the Russian Air Force after they repaired the aircraft following a landing accident four years earlier. It has seen intermittent service with Antonov Airlines ever since.

In 2009, the An-22 (now UR-09307) disappeared from view at Gostomel for a relaxed overhaul that lasted an impressive seven years. It reappeared in February 2016 and was later painted in Antonov Airlines' new colours. Already 32 years old, the unique Antonov is seen waking up the population of Toulouse in December 2006.

Back in Russia, consolidation was under way, and a few big players were starting to dominate the market. Vladislav and Natalia Filev, who had bought Sibir, were not content to run a regional operation in Siberia. Like many other proud new airline managers across Russia who suddenly had a sizeable fleet of large Tupolevs and Ilyushins lined up outside in the snow, they must have wondered what to do with them all. It was no secret that aircraft utilisation at many Aeroflot outposts had been extremely low.

Sibir's answer was to open a new base to the east in Irkutsk and another to the west at Domodedovo in Moscow. Gradually, more and more aircraft moved to Moscow, and in expansion mode Sibir bought the assets of Vnukovo Airlines and Baikal Airlines. Growth continued with Western aircraft, but some of the Soviet fleet lasted until 2008. Tu-154M RA-85635 heads an all-Soviet line-up in gloomy Domodedovo in May 2005.

Vladislav Filev is still the majority shareholder and CEO of the S7 Group. Asked to comment on Soviet-era airliners (in late 2020), he was very positive about the Il-86 – other than its insatiable appetite for fuel: 'The aircraft was very solid, had a high level of redundancy, was convenient for the crew and comfortable for passengers.'

Well experienced with the Tu-154, Filev was more critical: 'The aircraft was unforgiving for pilot mistakes, had an inflexible AMM (Aircraft Maintenance Manual), lack of MEL (Minimum Equipment List), and past century comfort standards.' But he liked the Tu-154 for its 'highest in class airspeed, essential for long Russian distances… good range, and plenty of space for cargo'.

Did Sibir take a close look at the Yak-42? 'Never,' said Filev. 'This aircraft's seating capacity is completely wrong for the Russian network – but that's just my personal view.'

Pulkovo Airlines, in St Petersburg, was another emerging powerhouse. However, its survival (and later merger with Rossiya) would revolve more around politics and the support of Aeroflot. The Leningrad operation had always been important for Aeroflot. Other than Moscow, Leningrad was the only city in the whole of the Soviet Union that merited a regular scheduled service (often just weekly) to most Western European capitals until the early 1990s. Nine Il-86s, 15 Tu-154s and 22 Tu-134s had been assigned to the operation.

The smart new Pulkovo Airlines identity featured the red St Petersburg crest next to the cockpit windows, as seen on two Tu-134A-3s at Pulkovo Airport in March 2005.

Unfortunately, Pulkovo lost Il-86 RA-86060 in a fatal crash at Sheremtyevo in July 2002, when the stabiliser deflected fully down just after rotation. The aircraft was on a ferry flight to St Petersburg, and no revenue passengers were on board. This was the only accident in the type's history, and marred an otherwise excellent safety record for the big Ilyushin. Pulkovo's Il-86s were inching towards retirement in 2005, including RA-86094 here in St Petersburg. This aircraft was broken up in 2010.

With the Tu-134s and Il-86s too noisy for most European destinations, the trusty Tu-154M – which just crept in under the wire – and 737s handled much of the Pulkovo international flying. By 2007, Pulkovo had merged with Rossiya within the Aeroflot group. Tu-154M RA-85204 is showing off its new Rossiya 'Russian Airlines' titles on short finals into Toulouse in June 2007. This aircraft is one of the many -154s that were repatriated to Russia from China in the early 2000s. Rossiya flew its last Tu-154 service in November 2009.

Rossiya the airline is sometimes confused with the Rossiya Special Flight Detachment (also known as the Special Flight Brigade or Squadron), tasked with flying Mr Putin and other government VIPs. Almost every Soviet jet airliner design has seen service with the Special Flight, with the notable exception of the Il-86 and Yak-42 (page 63). Today the fleet is focused on ten specially configured Il-96s and 13 Tu-204/214s. Tu-154M RA-85645 visited Toulouse in December 2007.

The old Aeroflot Novosibirsk and St Petersburg directorates would keep going in their different ways, but the outlook was not so good elsewhere across Russia. There had been two big UADs within Aeroflot's Far Eastern Civil Aviation Directorate, one in Khabarovsk and one in Vladivostok. In 1992, Dalavia Far East Airways took over the Il-62s, Tu-154s and An-24s in Khabarovsk, and Vladivostok Air did the same with the Tu-154s and Yak-40s in Vladivostok.

The Dalavia team must have been composed of seasoned Aeroflot veterans who saw no need to make radical changes to the colours of their aircraft, or do anything different from what Aeroflot had been doing for previous 30 years. The fleet even flew in full Aeroflot colours until 1998, when the 'new' Aeroflot in Sheremetyevo cracked down and told them they could not share the brand indefinitely. The Dalavia titles and logo were then applied to the basic old Aeroflot colours.

Il-62M RA-86131, one of the last -62s off the line and delivered in early 1993, is enjoying another relaxed day at its Khabarovsk base in May 2005. Tu-154B-2 RA-85477, delivered in 1981, had served all its life in the Soviet, and then Russian, Far East.

With massive debts, Dalavia was declared bankrupt in 2009. There was a short-lived and unsuccessful plan to incorporate all Dalavia's assets into a new government-sponsored airline called Rosavia, which would have been owned by the industrial giant Rostechnology. Most of the fleet ended up derelict in Khabarovsk. The Tu-154 was finally broken up in 2014, and the Il-62 the following year.

Vladivostok Air was less shy than Dalavia about introducing a new corporate identity, but it took a while. There was a common interest with Dalavia, in that both airlines procured Tupolev Tu-214s in the early 2000s. The Tu-214 was a shortened Tu-204 (just 142 seats in Vladivostok's layout), with additional range. It was capable of flying the prestige eight-hour non-stop route to Moscow from both Vladivostok and Khabarovsk. Vladivostok Air took advantage of the first delivery in 2003 to introduce a new livery, seen here on Tu-154M RA-85689 in Vladivostok in May 2005.

One of the Yak-40s in the background, RA-87273, is being prepared for a lengthy 850km sector across the Sea of Japan to the Japanese port city of Toyama. Vladivostok Air usually flew this schedule three times a week. The unhurried 32-seat Yak-40 would take over two hours to reach the Japanese coastline, but at least passengers had the reassurance of three engines for the long overwater crossing. Although the Yak-40 was first conceived as a 27-seater with nine rows of three seats, most operators ended up with much tighter four-abreast seating and 32 seats. Social distancing is difficult in a four-abreast Yak-40.

An efficient ANA ground team can be seen meeting the 33-year-old Yak (proudly named 'Vladivostok') in Toyama. It must have made a change from their usual routine of turning around 777s from Tokyo.

Aeroflot stepped in to acquire Vladivostok Air in 2013. The airline was then merged with SAT Airlines to create Aurora, a new subsidiary in the Far East.

There were other descendants of old Aeroflot directorates that were only going to last a few more years. Up in the barren landscape just below the Arctic Circle, and almost 1,000km north of Moscow, AVL Arkhangelsk Airlines had inherited a modest fleet of Tu-154s, Tu-134s, An-26s and An-24s from Aeroflot's Arkhangelsk directorate. By 2007 AVL had been reorganised as an Aeroflot affiliate called Aeroflot Nord.

Tu-134A-3 RA-65084, then 30 years old, is seen here enjoying the early morning sunshine far to the south, in Simferopol on the Black Sea, in July 2007. It would depart shortly to Sheremetyevo on an Aeroflot Nord flight, all 76 seats occupied. Simferopol was then in Ukraine, but would be back in Russian hands (with the rest of the Crimea) seven years later.

Far away in Krasnoyarsk, Kras Air was also running into financial problems. Unlike its Sibir neighbours in Novosibirsk, Kras Air had made less progress in diversifying its network and adding new bases. To try to achieve some critical mass, In May 2007 it joined up with Domodedovo Airlines, Samara Airlines, Omskavia and Sibaviatrans to form Air Union, but this venture collapsed in December 2008.

Tu-154M RA-85720, its tail half blackened with exhaust from its clamshell thrust reversers, is awaiting its passengers in snowy St Petersburg in March 2005. Only the -154M suffered from black tail syndrome. The Kuznetsov engines on earlier Tu-154s produced less smoke, and had cascade-type reversers that did not shoot the exhaust straight up the tail.

Despite its difficult past, in some ways it is surprising that the Yak-42 did not become more popular in the 2000s. Its high bypass Lotarev engines meant it was comparatively quiet and smoke-free. Unlike many of its Tupolev cousins, it could be operated anywhere. The 231st Flight of Aeroflot's North Caucasian directorate had operated a modest fleet of Yak-42s, Tu-134s and Yak-40s from Volgograd. The aircraft were transferred to newly formed Volga Airlines in 1992, which in turn became Volga Aviaexpress in 1998. Yak-42D RA-42384, configured with 120 seats, is departing Domodedovo for Volgograd in August 2009. Volga Aviaexpress only survived another year before filing for bankruptcy.

The North Caucasian directorate also included its 209th Flight at Mineralnye Vody, which became KMV, or Kavminvodyavia. The fleet was composed of Tu-134s, Tu-154s and two 195-seat Tu-204s. Unlike Volga Aviaexpress, KMV became fairly active in the Mediterranean charter market as well as its scheduled network. As a lucrative side business, it also operated Tu-154Ms for Iranian airlines. Tu-154M RA-85746 is also heading out from Domodedovo in August 2009. In another blow for the diminishing Soviet airliner population, the airline was shut down in 2011. Most of the Tu-154s had been broken up at Mineralnye Vody by 2013 – although 85746 survived until 2015.

Tatarstan Airlines and Izhavia were among the last airlines still flying the Tu-134. Both had adopted predominantly white colours, which suited the sleek Tu-134 well. Tatarstan's RA-65102 roars away from Domodedovo into stormy skies in August 2009, closely followed by Izhavia's RA-65056. Both aircraft would be retired within two years.

Little Izhavia, the 'national airline' of the Udmurt Republic, was based in Izhevsk in the Urals, some 1,200km southeast of Moscow. It had kept going with a handful of Tu-134s, Yak-42s, An-24s and An-26s since 1992 and would end up as one of the last airlines still flying the Yak-42. Izhavia is one of the few scheduled airlines in the world that has consistently achieved an average fleet age of over 30 years, although this interesting claim to fame is not mentioned in the company's publicity material.

It would have been impossible to imagine such a scenario just two decades earlier, but in the early 2000s Aeroflot was moving much closer to operating a fleet dominated by Western aircraft. It retired the last Il-62 in November 2001, and the Il-86 in November 2006. Next would be the Tu-134 and Tu-154, which followed in swift succession. Perhaps there was nothing that symbolised the demise of the great Soviet airliner more than the disappearance of these two workhorses from the Aeroflot fleet.

First to go was the Tu-134. Over 40 years since the aircraft's entry into service (from Moscow to Murmansk in September 1967, followed by the first international service to Stockholm three days later), Aeroflot retired the last 14 aircraft from regular duty on 31st December 2007. The final scheduled service was operated between Kaliningrad and Moscow that day. Over 600 Tu-134s had flown with Aeroflot. 'A Fail Safe and Infallible Vehicle' is how the airline described the faithful -134 on its retirement.

The last Tu-134s in service all received the new Aeroflot colours. Tu-134A-3 RA-65784, then 26 years old, is powering away from Sheremetyevo in April 2006. The crew had clearly not wasted much time in selecting 'landing gear up'. Tu-134A-3 RA-65717 (marked just as a Tu-134A) is on finals to Sheremetyevo in July 2007.

The Tu-154 was to bow out of Aeroflot service exactly two years later, on 31st December 2009. The final scheduled service was flown from Yekaterinburg to Sheremetyevo. The inaugural Tu-154 service had been from Moscow to Mineralnye Vody in February 1972, with the first international service to Berlin the following April. A total of 627 flew with Aeroflot between 1972 and 1991. ARIA continued to operate 42 Tu-154Ms from 1992.

Tu-154M RA-85135 is seen approaching the gate at Sheremetyevo in April 2006. Just like the Tu-134, the new Aeroflot colours suited the -154 very well. RA-85642, which had not been repainted, is also seen at Sheremetyevo. Several Aeroflot Tu-154Ms were originally delivered with the blue flash up the tail. The size and location of the flash suggested that its main purpose may have been to camouflage the familiar blackened lower tail.

The impressive Ilyushin 96 was intended to be the answer to Aeroflot's two biggest challenges on the long-haul network: range, and meeting all the rapidly changing noise and emissions legislation. Although generally similar in appearance to the Il-86, it was a different aircraft in many respects.

The initial Il-96-300 was five metres shorter than the Il-86. This had not been in Ilyushin's original plans, but (as in other Soviet projects) the engine became the constraining factor once again. The Il-96 and medium-haul Tu-204 were designed in the 1980s around the new Aviadvigatel PS-90A turbofan (once the Soloviev D-90A). The maximum 16,000kg of thrust offered by the PS-90A was not sufficient for the Il-86-sized, 350-seat aircraft that Ilyushin wanted to build, so the aircraft became a shortened 300-seater. Hence the '-300' designation given to the Il-96.

Like so many prototypes before it, the first Il-96 was assembled and then flew for the first time at Moscow's downtown Khodynka test airfield, in September 1988. It is a shame that Khodynka was closed in 2003. It must have been spectacular seeing a new widebody aircraft launch off the 1,700m runway almost in the middle of the city, bound for the long runway at Zhukovsky, deep in the woods of Ramenskoye in the outer suburbs.

As with the Il-86, series production of the Il-96 took place in Voronezh. Aeroflot flew the first Il-96 commercial service in July 1993, from Sheremetyevo to New York – JFK. The -96 really did have the long-haul capability Aeroflot had never quite attained with the Il-62, and much less so with the Il-86. Capable of carrying 65 tonnes of payload up to 11,000km, the new Ilyushin brought San Francisco and Los Angeles within reach of Moscow. RA-96010 is here at Sheremetyevo in April 2006, all ready to go.

Aware that the economics of the short-bodied, four-engined Il-96 would be in for a rough ride when up against the A330 and 777, Ilyushin's designers later stretched the fuselage back again – by nine metres, so longer than the Il-86 – to create the 350+ seat Il-96M and Il-96T freighter. The first Il-96M, powered by 17,000kg-thrust PW2337 engines in a collaborative venture with Pratt and Whitney, was unveiled in March 1993. The venture did not last long, and the renamed Il-96-400 ended up with upgraded PS-90A1 engines. Only five -400s have appeared so far, the last one as recently as 2020.

As for the Il-96-300, it did not fare much better. The six aircraft delivered to Aeroflot lasted little more than ten years in service. Aeroflot flew its last Il-96 service in March 2014, from Tashkent to Sheremetyevo. Three Il-96s went to Domodedovo Airlines and were broken up after the airline collapsed. Today, only Cubana intermittently flies an Il-96 on passenger schedules, and Rossiya's Special Flight Detachment has become the major operator of the type. Just 31 Il-96s have been built.

The Il-96's running mate with the new PS-90A engine, the Tupolev 204, also shared similar avionics, electrical systems and other equipment with the big Ilyushin. The Tu-204 flew for the first time in January 1989, and showed great promise for its future success as a replacement for the Tu-154 and for export markets. The 200-seater resembled a cross between a 757 and an A321, with a lanky undercarriage just like that of the 757.

In February 1996, Vnukovo Airlines operated the first revenue flight with the Tu-204, between Vnukovo and Mineralyne Vody. As with the Il-96, a Soviet design had transitioned into being a Russian aircraft. In 1992, the Russian government had ambitiously laid down plans for the production of 530 Tu-204s and 145 Il-96s by 2000. The intent was that these two new aircraft would be the flagships of all the major Russian airlines far into the future.

It was not to be. Aviastar, who ran the Tu-204 assembly line in Ulyanovsk, produced little more than two aircraft a year during the 1990s. There were many teething problems with both the airframe and the PS-90A engine. Aeroflot had stated it would order the Tu-204, but never did. Maybe it didn't help that there were 32 unscheduled engine changes on Aeroflot's Il-96 fleet in their first two years of service.

Perhaps Tupolev confused the market by introducing too many variants. There was the shortened, long-range Tu-204-300 (or Tu-214), built in a completely different factory in Kazan. Tu-214s were delivered to Rossiya's Special Flight Detachment, Transaero, Vladivostok Air and Dalavia. Then there was the very Westernised Tu-204-120, powered by Rolls-Royce RB211-535E4 engines, and delivered only to Air Cairo. And even a Tu-204C freighter as well. Little more than 60 Tu-204s were built in over 30 years. Regular Tu-204 passenger services in Russia came to an abrupt end in October 2018. Charter carrier Red Wings, citing the aircraft's limited service life, replaced its last five -204s with A320s.

Rolls-Royce-powered Tu-204-120 SU-EAF, arriving in Toulouse in May 2000, was delivered to Air Cairo in November 1998. It was one of two passenger and two freighter Tu-204s operated by the airline.

Dalavia's Tu-214 RA-64512, on finals to Sheremetyevo in July 2007 at the end of the long haul from Khabarovsk, had been delivered just a year earlier. Dalavia was only to survive another 15 months. The -214's career was brief on the long trans-Siberian routes for which it was intended. Vladivostok Air, with six Tu-214s, expanded rapidly in the Russian Far East after Dalavia's demise. But with only eight business and 134 economy seats, the -214s were just too small for the major transcontinental routes. Before Vladivostok Air stopped flying, it acquired an A330 to handle the high traffic volumes to Moscow.

Continuing issues with spares availability and the PS-90A engines did not help the Tu-204's reputation. Nevertheless, even if Aeroflot walked away from the -204, other major Russian airlines gave it a try. Sibir flew two Tu-204s in the early 2000s but did not take any more.

Transaero, once Russia's second biggest airline, flew three Tu-214s alongside its huge Boeing fleet for seven years, until the airline stopped flying in 2015. Alexander Pleshakov, who owned and ran Transaero with his wife Olga, said that the Tu-214s were in the fleet for 'insurance purposes'. The 'insurance', according to the Pleshakovs, was for the occasional official function when they might be introduced to President Putin. Mr Putin would always ask, 'I hope you are flying Russian airliners?' The Pleshakovs would answer, 'Of course, Mr President. They are simply the best!' Mr Putin would then nod approvingly and move to the next guests, perhaps not realising that Domodedovo Airport had become a Boeing showcase, bursting at the seams with Transaero 737s, 747s, 767s and 777s.

Tu-214 RA-64549 is under tow at Domododevo in August 2009. The Tu-154Ms in the background all belong to S7 or its subsidiary, Globus.

After more than ten years as the new 'Russian International Airlines', there were certainly some Aeroflot managers who thought that the airline should start to expand again beyond the confines of Sheremetyevo. Among the initiatives in the early 2000s was the creation of Aeroflot Don and Aeroflot Nord. Donavia had emerged in 1993 from another division of the old Aeroflot North Caucasian directorate, in Rostov-on-Don. It went bankrupt in 1998, and Aeroflot acquired a controlling stake in the assets. Aeroflot Don was formed in 2000, initially with Tu-134s and Tu-154s before moving to 737s.

Aeroflot Nord came later, in 2004, and was a rebranding of AVL Arkhangelsk Airlines (see page 82). The agreement came to a sudden end days after the fatal accident of an Aeroflot Nord 737 in Perm, in September 2008. In the meantime, several Tu-134s and Tu-154s flew in adapted Aeroflot 'Northern Lights' colours. Tu-134A-3 RA-65096 is at the gate at Sheremetyevo in July 2007 (with a Rossiya Tu-154 taxiing behind). Elderly Tu-154B-2 RA-85365, at 28 years of age and just a year younger than the Tu-134, is sharing the ramp with two Aeroflot Tu-154Ms while another one climbs away in the background.

Leaving a smoky haze in its wake, Aeroflot Don's Tu-154M RA-85149 taxies out for departure in Antalya in August 2009. This is another -154 that was repatriated from China. It is still wearing its basic China Southwest colours, six years after joining Aeroflot Don.

Aeroflot Don also scheduled some retired mainline Il-86s on key leisure routes in the summer. Aeroflot no longer flew its own Il-86 schedules, so was happy to operate the last few aircraft on the high-density, short-haul holiday routes where the big Ilyushin was in its element. RA-86103 has just arrived in Simferopol on the daily Aeroflot Don service from Sheremetyevo in July 2007. This was a morning flight, but the vodka had been out in force as a full load of happy holidaymakers headed for the sun. The atmosphere in the cabin gradually grew more raucous as the Ilyushin headed further south. It was really little different from an early morning departure on Jet2 from Leeds Bradford to Tenerife.

Passengers are milling around the forward and rear integral airstairs, a unique feature of the Il-86 that was not replicated on any other widebody other than customised VIP aircraft (including the Special Flight Detachment Il-96s). Passengers could leave excess hand baggage in a storage area on the lower deck before walking up the stairs to the main cabin. This all sounded fine but never really worked out. Apart from the confusion in identifying your bag, on arrival there was always the chance that someone getting off ahead of you would have taken a shine to your Tumi case or Louis Vuitton holdall. By the time you were out of your seat, they would have vanished through the terminal.

The Turkish resort of Antalya had become a favoured destination for Russians once they were free to travel overseas. Visas were not required to go to Turkey, and there were (and still are) hotels in Antalya that catered exclusively for visitors from Russia and other CIS countries. While their passengers did not need visas, the airlines did not need to meet any troublesome noise and emissions limits that would have banned their aircraft elsewhere.

This meant that Antalya, like Sochi and Simferopol on the Black Sea, and certain resorts in Egypt, became a great end-of-career destination for the Il-86 and older versions of the Tu-154. Atlant-Soyuz was one of the last operators of the -86. RA-86138, one of three aircraft then in the fleet, is taxiing out in Antalya in August 2009.

Set up by the City of Moscow in 1993 as its 'government' airline (as described in the small red titles under 'Atlant-Soyuz' on the Il-86, next to the city crest), the story of Atlant-Soyuz would probably make a good reality TV show. Up to 15 Il-76s were transitioned in and out of an ever-changing fleet, operating in all kinds of challenging environments outside Russia. Atlant-Soyuz seemed to have unusually excellent contacts with the Russian military, as it also leased in Tu-154s and Il-62s from the Russian Air Force for discreet 'charter' operations.

Ural Airlines is among the very few Russian airlines to have weathered the many crises, bankruptcies and consolidation of the 1990s and the last two decades. Like Sibir/S7, Ural expanded beyond its traditional base (Yekaterinburg) and flew extensively from other Russian cities. Three 350-seat Il-86s were dedicated to Antalya and other holiday hotspots. RA-86078 is thundering away from Domodedovo, also in August 2009. By the end of the year, just 13 Il-86s would still be flying commercially. They would all be grounded by May 2011.

Along with the Il-86s, Ural Airlines had always been a major Tu-154 operator since it took over Aeroflot's Urals CAD in 1993. Fifteen Tu-154B-2s were joined later by four Tu-154Ms, including the last-ever Tu-154 produced, RA-85833 (msn 1020). This aircraft was delivered new to Ural as late as June 2002, but had been completed in the Samara factory at least six years earlier. Ural undoubtedly obtained a great deal to take in aircraft that were already deemed obsolete.

Several of the last new Tu-154s took even longer to find a home. Two earlier aircraft, msn 997 and msn 998, were finally delivered to the Russian Air Force in August 2012 and February 2013. They had sat around, unloved and unwanted, in the Samara factory for no less than 18 years.

RA-85833 had the honour of being repainted in Ural's new corporate colours. As with several other airlines in Russia and the CIS, Ural took advantage of the arrival of its first Western jets (A320s) to roll out a new corporate identity. This last-ever Tu-154 is taxiing out under stormy skies at Domodedovo in August 2009.

RA-85844 (msn 992) was delivered new to Ural even later, in 2003, after languishing partially completed in Samara for seven years. The Tupolev looks rather forlorn on a half-completed taxiway at Domodedovo in May 2010, with Airbuses and Boeings now everywhere and just two Yak-42s barely visible in the far distance. The tug driver who parked the aircraft would certainly have had a bad night if he or she had accelerated by mistake in the last few seconds. RA-85844 was broken up just three years later.

Elsewhere at Domodedovo, there were aircraft less fortunate than Ural's busy Tu-154s. By 2009, the long, distinguished career of the Ilyushin 62 in passenger service was close to the end. The collapse of Domodedovo Airlines and the Air Union alliance had not helped, with a large based Il-62 fleet for which there was no further use. It was not long before there were at least 15 Il-62s pushed ignominiously onto the grass and waste ground across from the main terminal. Many would be slowly taken apart where they stood.

East Line, which owned and operated Domodedovo Airport, had invested in a massive new terminal and was keen to make the airport a worthy competitor to Sheremetyevo for international traffic. It always seemed an incongruous sight to look out from the gleaming new terminal and see many once-proud airliners sitting dismally on the grass across from the ramp. It was like going to a glitzy new Mercedes showroom, only to find a huge scrapyard for old Mercedes right in front of you.

East Line also operated a diverse fleet of aircraft. Founded in 1995, East Line Airlines managed to acquire or lease almost every kind of Soviet-designed aircraft imaginable, from a Tu-134 all the way to Il-86s. Many of the passenger aircraft – assorted Tu-154s, Il-62s and Yak-42s joined the fleet as well – only lasted a few months in service before being returned to their lessors. The cargo fleet fared better, and for a while East Line was a big player in the ad-hoc charter market. In 2003 the airline operated at least ten Il-76s. In May that year, Il-76TD RA-76403 has used up most of runway 14L in Toulouse as it begins a long slow climb-out.

East Line Airlines was acquired by the Russian Sky Group in 2004, which in turn became part of Vim Avia the following year.

Until the aircraft was banned in European skies, there was always a lively charter market for original Il-76s with Soloviev engines. Gazprom, which controls and manages all the natural gas in Russia, had operated a sizeable fleet of utility and cargo aircraft to support Russia's immense gas fields since 1995, including four Il-76s. It must have irritated many smaller operators when this wealthy organisation decided that its Gazpromavia subsidiary might as well earn some extra cash by chartering out these aircraft.

Gazprom often sponsors Russian participation at international events. In August 2000, it sponsored the Russian team at the world aerobatic championships in Muret, France. The team had the pleasure of travelling to nearby Toulouse in Il-76TD RA-76370, along with their two Sukhoi Su-26s. The Sukhois were reassembled right there under the Ilyushin's tail.

Ukraine had become a haven for the Yak-42 in the early 2000s. In 2003, there were six different airlines flying 30 of the big Yaks, but the numbers started to go downhill from then on. A 120-seat layout seemed to be standard for all the Ukrainian operators, a legacy from the original Aeroflot (and then Air Ukraine) configuration.

Dniproavia's Yak-42D RA-42419 is arriving in Frankfurt (opposite) in December 2000 on an early morning service from Dnepropetrovsk. Dniproavia lasted longer than most, until late 2017, when it was merged into Windrose Airlines by the common owner of both companies.

Donbassaero, like Dniproavia, was once also a division of Air Ukraine and, before that, Aeroflot's United Air Detachment in Donetsk. At one stage it had as many as 12 Yak-42s, but the fleet was winding down when UR-42318 was seen in Simferopol in July 2007. This aircraft was retired two years later. Donbassero moved on to a fleet of garish orange-red Airbuses, but went out of business in 2013.

Odessa-based Tavrey Aircompany was different, in that it was a private company and had nothing to do with Air Ukraine. Tavrey imported its three Yak-42s from Lithuania and Russia. UR-CER was also in Simferopol in July 2007.

While Yaks were on the decline, many Antonovs were enjoying a new lease of life. In the early 2000s, the sky was the limit for old Soviet-built freighters. In February 2008, in Miami, Florida, Avialeasing's An-26B UK-26003 was not shy about pointing this out. Given that the aircraft was registered in Uzbekistan but was flying on a regular cargo run from Miami to the Bahamas, maybe this 28-year-old veteran deserved its ambitious titles.

Avialeasing was founded in Tashkent in 1992 and grew a modest fleet of An-12s, An-26s and Il-76s. It sent a first An-26 to Miami in 2000, and (rebranded as SRX Transcontinental Inc.) an An-12 the following year. An avionics and component maintenance facility for the Antonovs was set up in 2004, the first (and only) of its kind in North America.

The An-26s proved more adapted to the Bahamas markets and routes within the Caribbean, and the An-12s flew much less. The An-12s ended up idle at SRX's Opa-Locka base for many years. Ukrainian-registered An-26 UR-GLS and An-12 UK-12002 were both at Opa-Locka in February 2008. The exhaust outlet for the An-26's Tumansky RU19A-300 booster turbojet (also installed on the An-24RV) can be seen in the An-26's starboard nacelle. At 900kg of thrust, this booster/APU delivered as much as 60% of the power of the basic AI-25 engine on a Yak-40.

Even as late as 2006, there were times when it was difficult to believe that it was the twilight era for the Soviet airliner. This is the north side of Sheremetyevo, home of Terminals 1 and 2 (now B and C), the Aeroflot maintenance base and the general aviation area, in May that year. It is hard to spot them, but there are five Yak-40s, a single Yak-42, 15 Tu-134s, ten Tu-154s, one Tu-204, three Il-62s, seven Il-86s, one Il-96 and a lone An-24. There is not a Western airliner in sight. On the other side of the runways, at the international terminal, the picture would be very different.

Just five years later, the Moscow airports would be dominated by Airbuses and Boeings. Even in the furthest reaches of Russia, there were few major airports where Soviet airliners were still hanging on in respectable numbers. One was Surgut, in Siberia, pictured here in June 2011 (see also pages 101 and 118). Two Tu-154s, eight Tu-134s, a lone An-24 and two Yak-40s (one on the grass) are making an impressive last stand. However, note the I-Fly 757 and Orenair 737-800 that have crept onto the scene.

Chapter 5

The Downward Slope – the Final Few Years

The decline of the great Soviet fleet accelerated rapidly from 2010. Consolidation and airline bankruptcies did not help. For the airlines still in business, increasing numbers of relatively new A320s and 737-800s were available at attractive lease rates, and so were A330s and 777s.

At the start of the new decade there was a handful of Il-62s and Il-86s still flying. An estimated 170 Tu-134s were still airworthy in Russia and the CIS, and another 60 with the military and elsewhere. Around 150 Tu-154s were reported to be operational in Russia and the CIS, and 20 more in other countries. This sounded fairly healthy, and in 2011, Tu-154s with Russian airlines flew 4.76 billion passenger-kilometres. However, this only represented 2.86% of Russia's total passenger traffic. By 2015, this figure had come down to a paltry 257 million passenger-kilometres, or just 0.11% of total traffic.

Even the Tu-154M, just noise compliant and a dependable stalwart for so many airlines, was coming to the end of the road. Kolavia's smart RA-85761, in rainy Surgut in June 2011, was in its last few months of service (see page 118). Gazpromavia held out with two aircraft until June 2016. Belavia operated its last service in October of the same year. Few would have predicted that a little-known Siberian airline called Alrosa would fly the last scheduled Tu-134 and Tu-154 flights ever, at least in Russia.

The era of the commercially operated Il-62 was almost over at the turn of the decade. Cubana had one last airworthy Il-62M, which was retired in March 2011. Air Koryo in North Korea had to stop flying Il-62Ms on its most prestigious international route to Beijing after the Chinese banned the aircraft for noise reasons at the end of 2012. The two airworthy Air Koryo aircraft were left to flying – very rarely – President Kim Jong-un, occasional domestic sectors and the groups of aircraft enthusiasts who went to North Korea just to sample the pleasures of the Il-62 and other Soviet-era airliners.

The Kazan Aircraft Production Association, which had taken over the Gorbunov factory where the Il-62 was built, converted three Il-62Ms to freighters in 2007. It set up its own airline, KAPO Aviakompania, to operate the aircraft. The Il-62MF (also known as the Il-62Gr) offered a 40-tonne payload, room for 12 pallets on the main deck and a large cargo door measuring 3.45m by 2m. RA-86576, a former Uzbekistan Airlines aircraft, is seen arriving in Domodedovo in October 2011. It is lowering its familiar Il-62 tail strut to ensure it does not tip over once it has parked.

The aircraft moved on to RADA Airlines in Belarus in 2015. Registered EW-450TR, it became a celebrity as the last Il-62 in regular commercial service. The long-term prospects for this lonely old Ilyushin seemed challenging. Few would have expected RADA to defy expectations and double its fleet five years later. But the airline did exactly that, faced with extra demand linked to the Covid-19 crisis. KAPO delivered one of the two other

low-time Il-62Grs to the airline late in 2020, now registered EW-505TR. These two unique survivors are also unusual in that they do not appear to have a base. 'As a charter airline we are planning to fly around the world without being tied to Belarus,' explained Dmitry Ischenko, RADA's commercial director.

The Russian Air Force's 223rd Flight at Chkalovsky continues to operate a handful of Il-62s. Il-62M RA-86555, showing off its sizeable communications antenna on top of the fuselage, was resplendent at Domodedovo in June 2014.

The faithful Ilyushin 18 was not doing much better than the -62. One old hand in Kazakhstan that had been around the tracks many times was Mega Air's Il-18GrM freighter UP-I1804, seen at Istanbul's Sabiha Gökçen Airport in October 2010. It had then been flying for 44 years. When the highly disciplined, politically correct East Germans at Interflug took delivery of this aircraft in July 1966, little could they have imagined that it would enjoy a later life in Poland and then the Middle East, with a colourful operation called Air Cess. The aircraft was registered in Swaziland and then Equatorial Guinea for good measure. The Il-18 made its way to Kazakhstan in 2002.

Fortunately, the Il-18 lives on with the military in various maritime patrol and electronic intelligence variants. Depending on the configuration, it can be called the Il-20, Il-22 or Il-38. An unidentified aircraft is seen in a far corner of the vast Zhukovsky complex in August 2013. It looks in great shape, maybe just out of overhaul and ready to be painted – all good news for the dwindling Il-18 population. A derelict Il-76, Yak-42 and Il-114 turboprop can be seen just behind.

When the photographer moved closer to investigate this mysterious Il-18, he was promptly arrested. At least the sensitivity around this old -18 was a good indication that it was not just a regular old airliner. The aircraft looks like an Il-38, configured for maritime patrol.

The Russian Air Force, and Rossiya's Special Flight Detachment at Vnukovo, have ensured that both the Il-18 and Il-62 have lived on beyond their commercial heyday. The huge base at Chkalovsky, to the northeast of Moscow, is certainly an Ilyushin haven – not to mention all the Antonovs and Tupolevs that are there as well.

This is the eastern apron at Chkhalovsky in May 2012. Eight Il-18s and five Il-62s can be seen on the ramp, not to mention two Tu-154s, nine Tu-134s, an An-12 and an An-72. Four very specialised Il-86s are tucked away with an Il-76 in their secret corner at the bottom of the photo. Packed with electronics, these famous Il-86VPUs, or 'Il-80s', are aerial command posts, and one or two are still reported to be airworthy today.

Over on the other side of the runways, there are seven more Il-18s and another Il-62. There are also 15 more Tu-134s, seven Tu-154s, 15 An-72s, six Il-76s, seven An-12s and two An-26s, some of which are just out of this view. The remarkable collection of old Soviet hardware at Chkalovsky seems to change little over the years, and this scene was not much different in early 2021. It is even possible that some of the aircraft had barely moved in the previous nine years.

After its respite late in its career taking holidaymakers southwards, the rest of the Il-86 fleet had all but disappeared. Russians clearly take the expression 'put out to grass' very seriously, because that's exactly where most Il-86s went before they were dismantled. It must have been quite a feat to tow the Il-86's 222-tonne empty weight onto the grass.

In March 2012, S7's RA-86091 and RA-86097, both of which had entered the fleet with the acquisition of Vnukovo Airlines, were enjoying the short season of Siberian grass in Novosibirsk.

Some 5,300km to the southeast, in Ho Chi Minh City, there were few reminders of the once-dominant Soviet fleet at Vietnam Airlines. One last Tu-134 was still left in the long tropical grass (and behind a wall) in June 2009, and so were VASCO's (Vietnam Air Services Company) two An-30s. The An-30 was little more than an An-24 with an extended glass nose, ostensibly for survey and mapping purposes. The first An-30 (converted from an earlier An-24) flew for the first time in August 1967, and it is thought that 123 were built in Kiev's factory and 473 at Svyatoshino.

While the gas-guzzling, noisy Il-86 had clearly come to the end of its days, it seemed much too early for the younger Il-96 to meet the same fate. There were no takers for Domodedovo Airlines' three Il-96s, and by May 2010, RA-96009 had joined the sad group of retired aircraft at Domodedovo, in the middle above. By August 2011, the rest of the Domodedovo Il-96 fleet – RA-96006 and RA-96013 – were slowly being taken apart as well.

Many of the original Il-76s were retired in the early 2000s. The Il-76's operating scope was hugely reduced with the new noise and emissions legislation. There were too many operators chasing after the limited business that was still up for grabs in the CIS, parts of Asia, the Middle East and Africa. Once in a while there would be special dispensation for a first-generation Il-76 to visit a European airport where the type was supposedly banned. Sky Georgia's Il-76TD 4L-SKL managed to sneak in to Toulouse in April 2010.

Sky Georgia had flown passenger schedules before transitioning into an all-cargo operator in early 2010, with three Il-76s. The airline went out of business the following year. Coincidentally, Sky Georgia's marketing tag line was 'Sky is The Limit…', a slight variation on Avialeasing's An-26 (page 98).

A characteristic of Russian-style maintenance has always been the amount of work that is performed outside. Here at Domodedovo in June 2014, Il-76TD RA-76363 'Vasili Molokov' is jacked up out in the elements and appears to be undergoing a wheel change. The engines are clearly being looked over as well. This smart Ilyushin is one of six operated by the Russian Ministry of Emergency Situations (MChS Rossii). The MChS fleet also includes a specially configured Il-62M with 114 seats, several Yak-42s and An-74s, numerous helicopters and the unique Beriev Be-200CHS jet-powered flying boat. As a paramilitary organisation, MChS does not seem to be in a rush to retire the Il-76s, so these aircraft will hopefully survive well into the 2020s.

MChS Rossii is reportedly in the queue for the much-modernised Il-76TD-90VD with PS-90AN engines (similar to those on the Tu-204 and Il-96) and updated avionics. This version, which meets the current ICAO noise and emissions standards, should ensure that the venerable Il-76 is around for many years to come. The -90VD's maximum payload is an impressive 50 tonnes, and with its 14,500kg-thrust PS-90As (compared to 12,500kg in the old Soloviev D30KP on the original Il-76) it has much more sparkling climb performance. The production rate has been surprisingly slow, with only one or two aircraft coming off the line each year since 2004.

Showing off its 20 wheels, RA-76511 is departing from Toulouse in October 2012, just five months after it was delivered to heavyweight cargo specialists Volga-Dnepr. It is one of five in operation alongside the company's well-known fleet of An-124s.

The only other commercial operator of the -90VD is Azerbaijan's Silk Way Airlines, with three in the fleet. 4K-AZ100 is visiting Toulouse in October 2017. Ilyushin must have had some sort of cosy relationship with a local glass manufacturer when they designed the cockpit and nose of the Il-76. There are 41 panes of glass in total, in many different shapes and sizes. If one cracked, the chances are slim that an average -76 operator would have exactly the right replacement on hand in the hangar.

The remarkable Antonov 124 does not look as though it will disappear from our skies any time soon, but as a design dating from the early 1970s, it certainly deserves a mention. First flown in December 1982, the An-124 created a sensation when it appeared at the Paris Airshow in June 1985. The following month, it carried a payload of 171 tonnes to an altitude of 35,000 feet. The previous year, the giant Antonov's only rival – the Lockheed C-5A Galaxy – had struggled to carry 110 tonnes to 7,000 feet. In May 1987, an An-124 (albeit with no payload) flew over 20,000km around the USSR's border in 25 hours 30 minutes, all on one tank of gas.

Fifty-five An-124s were built between 1982 and 2000, the first 20 in Kiev and the rest in Ulyanovsk. In addition, the single, famous six-engined An-225 was completed in Kiev's Svyatoshino factory in 1988.

Volga-Dnepr Airlines has consistently been the biggest An-124 operator since it began flying in 1991, with marketing support from HeavyLift in the UK in the first few years. Named after the great Volga and Dnepr rivers (and originally to be called Dnepr-Volga Airlines), the airline can be credited with saving the An-124 programme. In the chaos as the Soviet Union disintegrated in 1991, the newly renamed Aviastar factory in Ulyanovsk was out of money. The great and the good of the city of Ulyanovsk came together, including several managers from the factory, to create the airline and throw a lifeline to this remarkable aircraft.

RA-82047 is climbing away from Toulouse early one morning in September 2012, displaying its '20 years' anniversary logo. The same aircraft is seen at closer quarters in January 2017.

The first commercial operator of the An-124 (in 1989) had been the Antonov factory, through its subsidiary Antonov Airlines. Like Volga-Dnepr, Antonov Airlines suffered in the second half of 1992 when the US and some European countries banned the An-124 on the grounds it was a military aircraft, and not certified to fly commercially. Incredibly enough, the airlines and Aviastar won civil certification in three months, both for the airframe and its Ivchenko-Progress D-18T engines.

Other An-124 operators have come and gone, but Antonov Airlines and Volga-Dnepr have survived three decades. In 2020, Antonov was operating seven An-124s and Volga-Dnepr nine of 12 aircraft in the fleet. There will always be a market for the aircraft's outsize cargo capability, and unique capacity to carry satellites and the largest aero engines. However, with many aircraft approaching (or even over) 30 years of age, they will not go on for ever. An uncontained engine failure on a departing An-124 in Novosibirsk, in November 2020, led to a decision by Volga-Dnepr to ground its fleet for a few weeks. The complex relations between Russia and Ukraine are not helping either, with spare parts, manuals and various upgrades not flowing easily between the two operators.

UR-82029 is landing in Toulouse in February 2020, and four months earlier UR-82007 – the fifth aircraft built, and the oldest still flying – does not look its 31 years.

There were still no noise hassles to worry about in Russia and the CIS, but the population of airworthy Tupolevs was disappearing fast. One Tu-134 stronghold that lasted longer than most was western Siberia, where UTair was still flying 13 Tu-134s in 2011 under its 'UTair Express' brand. RA-65575's starboard D-30 engine was receiving some attention in Tyumen in May 2011. Then 32 years of age, this veteran Tu-134A-3 would be broken up in Rostov-on-Don four years later.

UTair, like S7 and Ural Airlines, has survived through many ups and downs to be one of the major forces in the Russian airline business. UTair started life in 1991 as TyumenAviaTrans, taking over Tu-134s, Tu-154s, Yak-40s, An-24s and many helicopters from Aeroflot's Tyumen CAD. The airline expanded well beyond its western Siberian base, and was rebranded UTair in 2002. UTair is the biggest helicopter operator worldwide, and works in many countries for the United Nations.

Even further north, Yamal Airlines is also a survivor. Founded in 1997 and based in Salekhard, almost 2,000km from Moscow and bang on the Arctic Circle, Yamal operated as many as nine Tu-134s alongside a couple of Tu-154s and a few An-24s and Yak-40s. RA-65916, flown with 68 seats, was in its 26th year of operation when seen at Domodedovo in August 2009. The Tupolevs would soon all be displaced by 737s.

While the Tu-134 was well on its way to retirement in airline service, it had enjoyed a growing career as a corporate jet. The cabin was a good size. The aircraft was well understood and easy to handle in Russia. Its rakish lines gave it a certain allure. It was certainly far, far cheaper to buy than a glittering new Gulfstream or Global (between 5% and 10% of the price, depending on the cabin installation). There were many wealthy, nostalgic Russians who also felt proud flying in their own personal Tupolev, even if it was no longer allowed to fly to many countries outside Russia.

RA-65608 was a 42-seat corporate jet flown by UTair, with the airline name written discreetly on the forward fuselage. This Tu-134AK had originally been delivered to the East German Air Force (disguised in Interflug colours) in 1975, and after various owners ended up with UTair in 2003. It was widely known at UTair as the 'TBJ', just to make sure everyone knew it was certainly not a Boeing Business Jet (737), but a Tupolev Business Jet. The handsome TBJ is gracing the ramp in Tyumen in May 2011. It was broken up four years later.

One of the last Tu-134s flying commercially has been Meridian Air's Tu-134B-3 RA-65737, on the move here at Vnukovo in August 2015. This was also previously a military aircraft, delivered new to the Soviet Air Force as a Tu-134UBL in 1981. The UBL variant has an extended nose resembling that of the Tu-22M3 'Backfire' bomber. It is used for training crews for both the Tu-22M2/M3 and the larger Tu-160 'Blackjack', with similar low-speed handling characteristics to both types. Despite the -134s high fuel burn and operating costs, it is infinitely cheaper to fly around the circuit than the big bombers.

With the Tu-134UBL an important asset in the Soviet and then Russian Air Force fleets, it is an enduring mystery how a few managed to escape and were converted to corporate aircraft. RA-65737 had its 'Backfire' nose removed and was civilianised in 2007. Meridian flies corporate charters with a

predominantly Western fleet of high-end business jets, but the rugged Tu-134 has proved its worth on old, rough Soviet-era runways, which are beyond the scope of today's more fragile corporate jets. Two other Moscow-based operators also chartered out corporate Tu-134s, Kosmos and Sirius.

There might have been a small number of Tu-134s flying in 2017, but at least there were still a few hanging around. Tu-134LL RA-65562, while in faded Aeroflot colours, was operated as a research aircraft from Zhukovsky for most of its career. In its later life, it was converted into a geophysical survey aircraft, hence the remains of a ventral survey pod under the fuselage. It was retired in the summer of 1999 but was still out to grass in Zhukovsky 18 years later, in July 2017 – looking eager to take to the skies again.

The last commercial flight with the Tu-134 in Russia was flown on 22 May 2019. Alrosa, the airline subsidiary of the Almazy Rossii Sakha diamond mining company, flew RA-65693 from its base in Mirny, high up in the Siberian wilderness, to Novosibirsk. Alrosa also flew RA-65907, another 'wolf in sheep's clothing', which had spent at least ten years with the Soviet military testing the fire control radar for the MiG-29K and -29M fighters. Its rear passenger door identifies it as a Tu-134AK. It joined Alrosa at its Moscow base in 1994 and is seen in Zhukovsky in August 2009.

The Tu-154 fleet was also winding down. UTair was the last of the Russian heavyweights to fly -154s, and still had 18 in the fleet as late as 2011. They would all be gone by the end of 2013. A 166-seat Tu-154M RA-85755 is taxiing out under some threatening Siberian clouds in Surgut in June 2011. It was broken up in Ufa two years later. In Tyumen, 640km to the southwest, three decommissioned UTair Tu-154s were already ominously lined up in front of another -154 and numerous Yak-40s that were out to grass.

Among the CIS countries, Tajik Air was the last national airline to operate the Tu-154. In 2011 it was operating four Tu-154Ms, a few Antonov twins and had leased in two elderly 737s and a 757. Somon Air, with a much newer 737 fleet and key routes to cities like Frankfurt, had gradually taken over as Tajikistan's major airline. EY-85717, arriving in Domodedovo from Dushanbe in August 2011, lasted another two years in service. Tajik Air went out of business in January 2019, perhaps not really moving with the times since emerging from Aeroflot's Tajik CAD 28 years beforehand.

Note the MChS Rossi Il-62M and a Polet Flight Il-96-400T freighter in the distance.

One of the last of the Kuznetsov-powered -154s to be retired was Orenair's Tu-154B-2 RA-85603. Originally delivered to the Soviet government in 1986, this aircraft was reported as retired in 2002. It seemed to have led a busy retirement, because seven years later it was certainly back in action here in Antalya. It was finally grounded in 2011.

Orenair, originally Orenburg Airlines, emerged in 1992 from Aeroflot's Orenburg detachment in the Volga CAD. The airline started off modestly with five Tu-134s, five Tu-154s, five An-24s and three Yak-40s. By 2008, Orenair was the second biggest charter carrier in Russia, with 737s arriving at a rapid rate and even 777s on the way. Perhaps the 777s were a step too far, and Orenair was merged into Rossiya in 2016.

Orenair's Tu-154B-2s lasted as long as many much newer Tu-154Ms. Continent was a short-lived operator in Vnukovo in 2010/11, and RA-85795 was out on the grass at Vnukovo in August 2015. It had been broken up by the end of the year. This 1994-build aircraft had spent several years out of service with a damaged spar following a hard landing, and so would have ended up with very low hours when it was retired.

Many later -154Ms ended up flying very few hours. Some aircraft were broken up after less than 3,000 hours flying time – not even a year's utilisation for this class of aircraft in typical airline service today.

Kolavia's Tu-154M RA-85761 *Kogalym* is sharing a very wet ramp with a company Tu-134, six UTair Tu-134s and a UTair Tu-154 (just behind) in Surgut in June 2011. Kogalymavia was founded in 1993 as a joint venture between a local oil company and the city of Kogalym, in the Tyumen region. The airline was operating as many as eight Tu-134s and seven Tu-154s by 2005, but the fleet started to reduce in the following years.

On New Year's Day 2011, Kolavia's Tu-154B-2 RA-85588 caught fire on the ground in Surgut as it was preparing to taxi out for take-off to Moscow. Three passengers died in the ensuing evacuation. An investigation determined that there had been an electrical short circuit forward of the engines, and as a result the remaining 14 operational Tu-154Bs in Russia were temporarily grounded. Kolavia stopped flying in September 2011, but reappeared in an ill-fated joint venture with TUI as Metrojet the following May.

It was not a great time for Tu-154s, with South East Airlines grounding its fleet three months after Kolavia. This followed an accident at Domodedovo in December 2010. Tu-154M RA-85744, once with Azamat in Kazakhstan (page 43), had departed Vnukovo for Makhachkala in the Caucasus, but diverted to Domodedovo after losing power in two engines. It was later established that the flight engineer had inadvertently shut off a fuel pump. Two of the 168 on board lost their lives in the crash landing.

South East's Tu-154M RA-85031 is seen taxiing out at Domodedovo in August 2011. South East was formerly Daghestan Airlines, and before that part of Aeroflot's North Caucasian CAD at Makhachkala. It flew three Tu-154s and two Tu-134s.

The honour of flying the last commercial Tu-154 flight in Russia fell to Alrosa, who (as with the Tu-134) had soldiered on for longer than anyone else with this imposing trijet. On 28th October 2020, Tu-154M RA-85757 flew its final service from Mirny to Novosibirsk, with 141 fortunate passengers on board. It was an amazing 52 years since the Tu-154's first flight, on 4th October 1968. As the airline's chief executive, Andrey Gulov, rightly said, 'Together with this legendary aircraft, a whole era of domestic aircraft construction is leaving.'

The Tu-154 was not universally popular, even in Russia. Its reputation has suffered from a poor safety record, although many of the accidents were not the fault of the aircraft itself. In 2010 there had been the well-publicised crash of a Polish Air Force Tu-154M in Smolensk, killing a high-powered delegation including the president, Lech Kacznyski. On Christmas Day 2016, a Russian Air Force Tu-154B-2 flew into the Black Sea after taking off from Sochi. The aircraft had just made a refuelling stop en route from Chkalovsky to an air base in Syria. All the 91 passengers and crew were killed, including 64 members of the military's famous Alexandrov Ensemble choir. The news stunned Russia.

After detailed investigations, pilot error was diagnosed as the cause of both accidents. Yet further damage to the Tu-154's reputation had been done, as had been the case in many other accidents when the aircraft itself had not been at fault.

Roman Pakhomov, a board member of Aeroflot and closely associated with the management of Rossiya's Special Flight Detachment, said in October 2020 that the Tu-154 was his least favourite of all the great Soviet airliners. 'The reason is simple – the aircraft has one of the worst (worldwide) ratings for accidents per number of flight hours. It has a lot of issues in its design, the high speed on approach, poor safety of fuel lines, etc. Having three engines she could barely fly with one engine off. Fuel consumption was terrible – 4.5 tonnes of fuel per flight hour minimum.'

On a positive note, pilots loved the Tu-154's speed and agility. There were also incidents when the -154's structural integrity saved many lives. Alrosa's very own Tu-154M RA-85684 is being pushed back to a parking stand at Domododevo in May 2010. Four months later, this same aircraft made a forced landing on the 1,300m runway at the abandoned airport of Izhma, in the middle of nowhere 1,400km to the northeast of Moscow.

The -154 had suffered a total electrical failure in the cruise from Udachny to Domodedovo. Among other issues, this meant that the fuel pumps no longer worked, and the aircraft was left with 30 minutes of flying time. It overran the short runway and ended up in the undergrowth well beyond. All of the 81 occupants walked away unscathed, and the Tupolev underwent minor repairs and was flown out.

The famous Ilyushin and Tupolev jets were mostly gone by the end of 2020. Fortunately it was not yet the case for the small Yak trijets, and certainly not for the old Antonov freighters. The Yak-40 had established itself as a cheap and cheerful corporate jet across the CIS, rugged and dependable and at home flying into remote, austere airfields. As long as you didn't want to get anywhere fast and fuel prices were low, the Yak was just fine. RA-87828, originally delivered to Aeroflot in 1972, had been around for 39 years when seen here at Vnukovo in May 2011. The aircraft had more recently flown with Rusline, but it was thought a private operator had applied the distinctive polar bear image on the tail.

The Yak-40 has also been used as a test vehicle by several companies. KRET, a subsidiary of the giant state company Rostec, has used Yak-40K '87938' as a development aircraft for its radio-electronics business. The Yak was at Zhukovsky in July 2017.

The Russian Ministry of Internal Affairs (MVD Rossii) flies this smart Yak-40K RF-88301, resplendent at Zhukovsky in August 2011. The 'RF' (Russian Federation) registration prefix denotes its paramilitary role. The white bump on top of the fuselage doubtless has a special communications function, but it seemed wise not to ask the secret police exactly what it was for.

The MVD Yak started life with CSA in Czechoslovakia in 1977, and so did EW-464PS (two years earlier). This aircraft flew as a corporate transport for the Orsha Aircraft Repair Plant in Belarus from 2016 to 2018, leased from Motor Sich in Ukraine. The Orsha plant specialises in overhauling military Mil helicopters and also the Il-76. The Yak is making a quick visit to Zhukovsky in July 2017, showing off its autonomy on the ground with the sturdy ventral airstairs. The airstairs on the Yak-40 resemble little more than a thick metal plank cut out of the fuselage, with the steps welded together on the other side. This rustic approach has probably meant that these airstairs have survived on the airframe for all its 42 years.

The much bigger Yak-42 may have been considered a black sheep by some in the industry, but a few were still going strong in 2020. KrasAvia, owned by the administration of the Krasnoyarsk Region, was flying nine. Izhavia was also flying nine and even thinking about adding one or two more from the fleet of bankrupt Saratov Airlines. However, 737s were on the agenda as well. In 2018, Izhavia's president, Alexander Sinelnikov, had pronounced his -42s 'as reliable as Kalashnikovs'. This unusual comparison probably comes naturally in Izhevsk, as the Kalashnikov factory is located there.

RA-42455, arriving at Domodedovo from Izhevsk in September 2016, was one of eight Yak-42Ds that were originally delivered to China in the early 1990s. It joined Izhavia in 2010 and flies with a 104-seat two-class cabin.

Perhaps the most unusual Yak-42 still flying is '42440', flown by the Siberian Aeronautical Research Institute (SibNIA) for the Federal Service for Hydrometeorology and Environmental Monitoring of Russia, or Roshydromet. This Yak-42D (also referred to as a Yak-42LL) is a flying laboratory capable of measuring

radiation, air and land pollution, icing, cosmic rays and a host of other atmospheric conditions. There are 76 instruments on board and no fewer than 50 sensors, which do little to enhance the clean lines of the -42. The aircraft was parked at Zhukovsky in July 2017, awaiting a mission to drought-stricken Cuba to try to create rain with its cloud-seeding equipment.

The Antonov turboprops seem set to outlive almost all the Soviet-era jets, perhaps with the exception of some newer Il-76s and a few surviving Yak-40s. The oldest aircraft in Motor Sich's diverse fleet is An-24RV UR-MSI, here taxiing to its stand at Vnukovo in August 2015 after a two-and-a-half-hour flight on its scheduled service from Zaporozhye, in Ukraine. The veteran Antonov had originally been delivered to Aeroflot in March 1972.

Motor Sich Airlines was created in 1984 as a subsidiary of the huge Motor Sich aero engine company in Zaporozhye. Among thousands of other engines, this Antonov's Ivchenko AI-24 turboprops would have come from the Zaporozhye factory. Motor Sich's passengers can always be confident that the engines outside the window must receive the best tender loving care.

Southern Sky's An-24RV UP-AN424 was on the Kiev production line at just the same time as Motor Sich's Antonov, so was not far from its 48th birthday as it taxied at high speed in Nur Sultan (previously Astana), Kazakhstan, in October 2019. This aircraft has served in Kazakhstan all its long life. Southern Sky is the turboprop operation of SCAT (page 73).

Everything seemed to be holding up well for the airworthy An-12 population until late 2019. For many years, two Ukrainian airlines, CAVOK Air and Ukraine Air Alliance, had consistently found ad-hoc work almost everywhere in the world for their Antonovs, just as their Bulgarian predecessors had done until 2007. The An-12 was relatively cheap to hire, offered a payload of close to 20 tonnes and could fly up to 5,000km. For one-off charters carrying bulky loads, there was nothing quite like it on the market.

By 2019, some of the aircraft in the Ukrainian fleets were well over 50 years old. They took marathon transatlantic missions in their stride. CAVOK's 1972-build An-12BP UR-CKM was a comparative youngster. It is storming into Toulouse non-stop from St John's, Newfoundland, in October 2019.

On 4th October 2019, Ukraine Air Alliance lost An-12 UR-CAH when it ran out of fuel just short of the runway on the approach to Lviv, en route from Vigo in Spain to Istanbul. Shortly afterwards, the airline was banned from flying to Europe and then grounded by the Ukrainian authorities. CAVOK consequently faced restrictions as well. At the time of writing these airlines are back flying again, but under increased regulatory pressure. It is unclear for how long they can continue flying the An-12. A few other carriers, like Ruby Star in Belarus and Motor Sich, also offer a handful of An-12s for charter, but the days seem to be numbered for this remarkable aircraft… just as they are for all the other iconic Soviet airliners that are still hanging on. The era is truly coming to an end.

Epilogue

Airliners from the Soviet era have often been criticised for their safety record and limited environmental credentials. Much of the criticism is misplaced. It is easy to forget just how many were built in the first place, and that their designs date back more than half a century. The vast majority of accidents have come down to crew error, often in harsh operating conditions.

The longevity of many Soviet designs has been incredible. Whether it be in the Chukotka peninsula or in Kazakhstan, there will soon be An-24s that have been consistently flying the same routes, day in and day out, for 50 years. Not many aircraft, buses or boats manage that. There are very few years left for these rugged turboprops, but the family will live on with the An-26 and An-32.

If it wasn't for their noise and off-the-wall fuel consumption, some low-time Tu-134s and Tu-154s would have lived on as well. They are just as robust as the Antonovs. The author once experienced the hardest landing of his life – more of a controlled crash – in a Tu-134 that was caught in severe wind shear just before touchdown. After two minutes of hesitation at the end of the runway, the shaken crew collected their thoughts and taxied the aircraft to its stand. The Tupolev was subjected to a thorough structural check two days later, and after some repairs lived on to fly again. Other contemporary aircraft might not have survived, with the very real possibility that the undercarriage would have been forced up through the wing.

While the commercial outlook for the big jets is bleak, the military will keep them in the air for a while yet. It is difficult to imagine the Russian Air Force sourcing a big fleet of A320s, 737s or even home-grown MS-21s for transport duties any time soon. With the last Tu-154 delivered as recently as 2013, much of the fleet still has lots of flying hours left. There is no easy replacement for the Tu-134UBL bomber trainers, which are expected to remain in service until at least 2023.

However, the sight of a flying Tu-134 or Tu-154, let alone an Il-62 or Il-86, is now a rare event. The same will soon be true for the Yak-42, but a few resourceful operators should keep some Yak-40s going for a while.

The sun is setting on all these wonderfully charismatic aircraft, just as it has set on many of the airlines who have flown them. The sights, smells, noise, smoke and unique in-flight experience of these tremendous designs will not be easily forgotten.

The impressive long line-ups of Soviet-era aircraft, sometimes idle for weeks at their base, will also not be forgotten. Uzbekistan Airways Tu-154B-2 UK-85600 (last seen on page 41) is heading a line-up again in Tashkent eight years later, in March 2006. It flew very little in all those eight years, but at least enjoyed a visit to the paint shop to receive regular airline colours.